The Clydesdale

The Clydesdale

workhorse of the world

Mary Bromilow

ARGYLL ✣ PUBLISHING

Argyll Publishing
Glendaruel
Argyll PA22 3AE
Scotland
www.argyllpublishing.com

British Library Cataloguing-in-Publication Data.
A catalogue record for this book is available from
the British Library.

ISBN 978 1 906134 65 5 hardback

Printing: Bell & Bain Ltd, Glasgow

In memory of my parents and grandparents,
where it all began.

As Patron of the Clydesdale Horse Society, I am delighted to welcome this new and very beautiful tribute to Scotland's Clydesdale horse, not least because I find myself following in the footsteps of my great-great-great grandparents, Queen Victoria and Prince Albert, who each held the Patronage of the Society.

For two hundred years, these magnificent heavy horses have been an important part of our history. Such is the depth of our relationship with the Clydesdale that now, in the twenty-first century and, rather against the odds, they are rediscovering new levels of popularity across the world.

However, when you think back just sixty years, it is terrifying to consider how close we came to losing them forever. In 1946, there were two hundred working Clydesdales in this Country. Just three years later, that number had fallen to just eighty and today, despite a resurgence in their popularity, they are still categorized as "at risk" by the Rare Breeds Survival Trust, of which I also happen to have been Patron for many years.

Today, however, I am increasingly heartened by the renaissance which the working horse appears to be enjoying. As Patron of the British Horseloggers Society, I know that the Clydesdale is a very popular choice of horse, strong and with the perfect temperament. Moreover, using horses is so much better for our environment, particularly in terms of woodland management, but also in other ways where man is working with animals and delivering profound psychological benefit.

In recent years, I have been doing whatever I can to raise awareness of the relevance of working horses in our own era, particularly on the steeper sites and those of real sensitivity where horses do so much less damage than those huge machines which leave ugly scars on the landscape, causing immeasurable damage to biodiversity. It seems to me that horses fit so well into the whole process of conservation and woodland management and I can only urge anyone involved with woodlands to give every consideration to using horseloggers.

The history of the Clydesdale is very much part of our Island story, their lives being so intimately interwoven with the lives of those farming families who worked with them over the generations. They are very special animals and as you read this book perhaps, like me, you will call to mind those most moving words of Ronald Duncan who, in 1954, wrote of the horse:

"Where in this wide world can man find nobility without pride,
Friendship without envy,
Or beauty without vanity?
Here, where grace is served with muscle
And strength by gentleness confined
He serves without servility; he has fought without enmity.
There is nothing so powerful, nothing less violent.
There is nothing so quick, nothing more patient."

Jim Thomson, Ingleston, Moniaive, with a 3-horse binder at the
Millenium Horse Show, Kittochside, South Lanarkshire, 2000
Photo John Zawadzki

Contents

The horses on the Great Clydesdale Migration line up for feeding
Courtesy of Cumbrian Heavy Horses

Stallion in the snow
Heavenly Benedictine of Arclid
ridden at home in Sweden
Courtesy of Little Big Ranch

Introduction

I WAS lucky enough to be growing up in the years following World War II, when the Clydesdale horse was still in common use in rural Scotland. My love for horses has been life long, and it began for real in my early childhood when I would stop anything I was doing to watch the horses. The connection went back to before I was born, when my grandfather William Crawford had been a stud groom and stallion man for Albert Marshall at Bridgebank, Stranraer in the 1920s. It must have been in the blood, for my parents waited in vain for me to 'grow out' of them, and I have had horses, although not Clydesdales, continuously since I was fifteen years old.

Although Scotland has produced many excellent native

breeds of livestock, the Clydesdale is unique in the extent of his influence and the lyrical praise heaped upon him from sources all over the world. This magnificent, beautiful, honest and noble animal has touched the lives of people from all walks of life over the last two hundred years, has survived virtually critical reductions in numbers, and come back in the early twenty first century to unimagined levels of popularity in industries and uses undreamed of a hundred years ago.

The idea for this book grew out of the realisation that, although works had been published in other countries, nothing had been produced in the Clydesdale's native land for almost thirty years, since Eric Baird wrote *The Clydesdale Horse* in 1982.

We should be so proud of the Clydesdale horse, which, like 'auld Scotia' of the Robert Burns poem, is 'loved at home, revered abroad,' and whose roots are so firmly planted in the fertile soil of South Lanarkshire.

I hope this illustrated tribute will do justice to this much loved heavy horse, and make interesting reading for anyone who, for whatever reason, feels that admiration and affection whenever a Clydesdale passes by.

Mary Bromilow
Thornhill, Dumfriesshire
January 2011

And the white and honest faces,
The power upon the traces,
Of the Clydes!
Courtesy Victor Harbor Tramway

CLYDESDALES

The Suffolk Punch will keep the road;
The Percheron goes gay;
The Shire will lean against his load
All through the longest day;
But where ploughland meets the heather
And earth from sky divides.
Through the misty Northern weather,
Stepping two and two together,
All fire and feather,
Come the Clydes!

The Hunter gallops on the lea,
The Garron treads the ling,
The Hackney, touching nose and knee,
Will make the roadway ring;
But, apart from play and pleasure,
With the sweat upon their sides,
Where the furrow is to measure,
And the earth to turn for treasure,
Serfs of little leisure,
Go the Clydes!

To each the favourite of his heart,
To each his chosen breed,
In gig and saddle, plough and cart
To serve his separate need!
Blue blood for him who races,
Clean limbs for him who rides,
But for me the giant graces,
And the white and honest faces,
The power upon the traces,
Of the Clydes!

Will H. Ogilvie from *The Collected Sporting Verse of Will H. Ogilvie* Constable and Company Ltd. London 1932

DESPERATE DAN © DCTHOMSON&CO.,LTD

Desperate Dan
Courtesy of D C Thomson & Co.Ltd

1. Plough to Pestalozzi Street: from humble servant to celebrity

ASKED for their memories of Clydesdales, most people in this country recall the working horses of the past. Pulling and sweating over the headland with the plough, their white legs dark with earth. Plodding the city streets in days gone by, carting coal, and hauling materials for heavy industries, or loads from harbours such as Aberdeen. Younger folk will quote the mechanisation of farming and the dwindling numbers in the local Agricultural Shows, which might suggest that Clydesdales have had their day.

Few images encapsulate the combination of power and gentleness better than the working Clydesdale. In the words of Ronald Duncan's tribute:

> Where in this wide world can man find nobility without pride,
> Friendship without envy, or beauty without vanity?
> Here, where grace is laced with muscle,
> And strength by gentleness confined.
> He serves without servility, he has fought without enmity.
> There is nothing so powerful, nothing less violent.
> There is nothing so quick, nothing more patient.
> All our past has been borne upon his back.
> All our history is his industry.
> We are his heirs, he our inheritance.

These working horses are woven into the fabric of our social history, and their humble, often harrowing daily toil was lived out alongside the men and women who populated the towns and cities, farms and villages.

Carnera with Falkirk Stableman
John Corson, who was
6feet 3 inches tall
Courtesy of A G Barr plc

An early example of a Clydesdale 'celebrity' was Carnera, who was owned by A.G. Barr, makers of the soft drink Irn Bru. Standing 19 hands 2 inches tall, he was bought as a five-year old by Robert Barr in 1930 from a Perth farmer for £80. Believing him to be 'the biggest horse in the world', he was named after Primo Carnera, the Italian boxer who became the World Heavyweight Champion. With a shrewd eye for a promotional asset, Robert Barr was proved right. Carnera became famous as he hauled a flat-top lorry, loaded with crates, around Falkirk and district over the next six years. Living up to the legendary strength of his namesake, the lorries he pulled carried up to 70 dozen bottles and weighed about three tons. He was regularly fed buns by the shoppers in the High Street, which was his regular route. And gentle giant that he was, he relished the attention.

Sadly, in January 1937, Carnera slipped on the icy road in Cow Wynd and broke his pelvis. For more than four hours his driver, Bill Fotheringham, and a local vet, tried to raise him, while a crowd of sympathetic onlookers gathered. Mattresses were brought from a nearby furniture store, and, according to Robert Barr, weeping girls were queuing to give him buns as he lay on his side. 'And he didn't let them down. He ate every one.'

Such was the crowd that had gathered that three policemen were needed to keep control of the traffic. And the crowd did not disperse until Carnera's body was loaded on to a lorry and taken away at 7pm.

The Clydesdale's inclusion in Scottish popular culture was demonstrated by D.C. Thomson, publishers of *The Dandy* comic. Desperate Dan, the Cactusville cowboy, made his debut as a character in the first edition of *The Dandy* in 1937. As a baby he had a ten-gallon baby bonnet, a matching twelve-gallon nappy, spurs on his bootees and a horse-drawn pram. He grew big and strong on his Aunt Aggie's cow pies, and you only need to look at his horse to see that only one breed was strong enough for the boy whose skipping caused an earthquake.

A local hero of a different kind was Jimmy. The Reverend Callum O'Donnell, Minister of Southend Parish Church at the southern tip of the Kintyre Peninsula, came up with a novel way of travelling around his widely scattered flock during his tenure from 1997 to 2000. Before arriving, he bought an 18 hands 10 year old Clydesdale who had just spent the previous few years as a forestry horse. Soon the horse was known locally as the 'Rev. Jimmy', and was much more than a mode of transport. He was not only popular with the older folk, in whom he sparked off fond memories of life before mechanisation, but the children, who thought he was the star of the parish. On his visits to the local primary school, he didn't stop in the playground. 'He has his own form of ministry,' said Mr. O'Donnell.

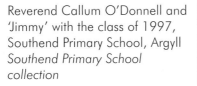

Reverend Callum O'Donnell and 'Jimmy' with the class of 1997, Southend Primary School, Argyll
Southend Primary School collection

Jim Steel's Clydesdales from Jackton, East Kilbride, preparing to transport the guests at Stella McCartney's wedding on Bute in 2003
Press Association

It was also in Argyll, on the Island of Bute in 2003, that teams of Clydesdale horses were called in to transport the celebrity guests of the wedding of fashion designer (and Beatle Paul's daughter) Stella McCartney. The wedding took place at Mount Stuart House, home of the 7th Marquis of Bute, whose family are direct descendants of Robert the Bruce. Strict privacy arrangements were in place, and even John McMillan, the local contractor and Clydesdale breeder who co-ordinated the carriage arrangements with Hugh Ramsay and Jim Steel, was not allowed to carry a camera on the day. However, the Press Association, who had scented a celebrity occasion, had sent photographers to capture what they could. And the eight Clydesdales, who had arrived from as far away as Galloway, were the image of the day.

John McMillan's Clydesdales had also been centre stage at Her Majesty the Queen's Golden Jubilee Parade in London on 4th June 2002. Two of his Clydesdale geldings, Bobby and Sandy, travelled to London to pull the 1860 built Coastguard Wagon. Coastguard Officers, and Coastguard Rescue Team members in 1950s clothing, joined the wagon and horses in the 'Yesterday' section of the parade to head up the Maritime and Coastguard Agency contribution.

John McMillan's Clydesdale geldings Bobby and Sandy head the Maritime and Coastguard Agency wagon for Her Majesty the Queen's Golden Jubilee Parade in London in 2002
Photo Sandra Clark

Who would have thought that Scotland's humble work horse would take part in not one, but two United States Presidential Inaugural Parades? Such was the popularity of the Budweiser Clydesdales that they were chosen participants in the parades for President Harry Truman in 1949, and 44 years later, in 1993, for President Bill Clinton.

Budweiser Clydesdales in Harry Truman's Presidential Inaugural Parade in 1949

On 7th April 1933, to celebrate the end of Prohibition, August A. 'Gussie' Busch, Jnr. sent two six-horse hitches of champion Clydesdale horses trotting down Pestalozzi Street to draw up outside the Anheuser-Busch Brewery in St. Louis, providing such a spectacular surprise gift for the elderly August A Busch, Snr. that it reduced him to tears. Their role in the

Clydesdales deliver the first post prohibition crates of Budweiser beer to President Franklin D. Roosevelt at the White House in 1933
Used with permission of Anheuser-Busch, Inc. All rights reserved

celebration continued with one hitch being despatched to New York by train to make a special ceremonial presentation of a case of beer, outside the recently built Empire State Building, to former New York governor Al Smith.

From there the same hitch was transported by rail to Washington, D.C., where they made another special delivery of beer to President Franklin D. Roosevelt at the White House.

These ceremonial deliveries marked the start of the Budweiser tours of the United States that continue to this day. Clydesdales are the goodwill ambassadors for Anheuser-Busch, and have achieved international media fame through the Super Bowl promotional advertisements which are watched by countless thousands on the internet.

Boris the Clydesdale
Walker family collection

Boris was a 19 hands Clydesdale gelding, owned by George Walker of Inverurie, Aberdeenshire. Bought as a 3 year old from Orkney in 1985, Boris became a veritable star when he appeared in the TV soap 'Emmerdale' and his own series of four children's books. He also appeared in Mel Gibson's film version of 'Hamlet', but he will be best remembered as the children's favourite who was instrumental in raising over £2 million for charities such as The Grampian Children's Cancer Research Fund and The Anthony Nolan Trust. He was a regular visitor to the Aberdeen Sick Children's Hospital, where, as George Walker recalls 'he put smiles on children's faces.' One of his many celebrity duties was pulling a wagon load of whisky parcels for Japanese VIPs at the Glen Garioch Distillery anniversary.

He earned his hero status when, in 1999, a car smashed into the wedding carriage he was pulling in Westhill, Aberdeen. George, who was driving, believes that Boris saved the lives of the bridal party that day, as he lay unmoving in the road until freed from the harness, when most horses would have bolted. Having suffered a punctured lung, broken ribs and a broken collarbone, George was taken to hospital thinking that Boris was dead. The hospital switchboard was jammed with calls, not asking after George, but Boris, and the gift of sweets handed in by an old lady were also for the equine hero.

Boris retired from public life after the accident, but received letters, gifts and visitors right up to his death in 2008 at the age of 24. His shoe still hangs behind the bar at the Woolpack in 'Emmerdale'.

Ted Clydesdale is a big personality with his own web site, www.thestoryofted.com. Bought as a foal in 1998 by Sally Anne Oultram, he has grown to be a hugely popular guest at charity events following the publication of the children's book of the same name. In 2004 a raffle took place for a traditional wooden rocking horse, with leather harness, modelled on Ted. The rocking horse toured all the major equestrian events that year, with tickets on sale at £1. The tour and raffle raised £7,750.00 for the Rare Breeds Survival Trust, and Sally Anne and Ted were made the Trust's first ambassadors in 2010.

Ted Clydesdale with his owner
Sally Anne Oultram
Oultram family collection

Collessie Cut Above
Photo courtesy of R. Black

The Scottish Equestrian Association makes awards annually to outstanding names in the world of horses. But in 2005 the Lifetime Achievement Award, for the first time, went to a horse. The Clydesdale stallion Collessie Cut Above, a 17.3 hands bay foaled in 1992 and owned by Ronnie Black from Ladybank in Fife, won the 1997 Cawdor Cup and has gone on to breed Clydesdales that have won significant championships in every country in the world where Clydesdale horses are found.

The Breeder of the Year Award for 2009 went to Hugh Ramsay, whose Millisle Clydesdales have gained international acclaim, and who is also a widely respected judge in Europe and North America. He has judged the Clydesdale World Championships, but is perhaps best known as a driver of incredible skill, whose demonstrations at the Horse of the Year Show have won standing ovations. Crowds gather to watch him and as the following poem illustrates, never forget the spectacle.

SIX HORSE HITCH

On the fourth of August 'seventy-nine
A grand experience was mine.
I took a trip and made my way
To Perth's Fair City by the Tay.

I found my journey well worth while,
I saw Hugh Ramsay from Millisle,
A handsome, hefty, husky bloke
Exhibiting a six-horse yoke.

With harness bright and bells a-jingle
They fairly made the heart strings tingle;

Hugh Ramsay and his six horse hitch at the Royal Highland Show 2009
Photo John Zawadzki

A sicht to cure een that are sair,
Five gallant geldings and a mare.

As round the ring those Clydesdales sped,
The South Inch trembled 'neath their tread;
They ambled, trotted, cantered, strolled,
And always perfectly controlled.

A great display of horsemanship,
With quiet commands, no lashing whip;
A spectacle of grace and style
That beats Rolls Royce by a mile!

With expertise Hugh fairly sparkled
As round the field he weaved and circled;
For equine lovers what a treat,
Right well he graced the driving seat.

When finally they faced the stand
The applause was loud, prolonged and grand.
They well deserved that hearty cheer,
I hope they'll come again next year.

Geordie Rodger

'Some boys love dogs.'
Angela Davidson's son Lawrie with George and Ruth Skinner's gelding Jake
Image by kind permission of Angela Davidson Art

Actress Joanna Lumley tries her hand at ploughing, Ellisland Dumfries 2009
Photo: Ronnie Cairns

At George and Ruth Skinner's Strathorn Farm Stables in Aberdeenshire, you will find a truly versatile celebrity horse by the name of Sir Lancelot of Strathorn, also known as Jake. Not content with herding sheep, being driven in a unicorn and team, and showing at the Royal Highland Show in side-saddle, Jake is now the centre of attention as a model for Angela Davidson's stunning paintings of horses. Pictured with Angela and Sandy's son Lawrie, with the title 'Some boys love dogs', Jake's portrait is the perfect advert for the gentle Clydesdale and his empathy with children.

Ruth Skinner, MBE, with Lothian &
Borders Police horses 'Jim' and
'Mac', 2009
Skinner family collection

Strathorn Lady May, Drum Horse
for the Sultan of Oman
Skinner family collection

And the same family stables sold a Clydesdale mare to the
Sultan of Oman as a Drum Horse for the Millennium Celebrations, and two of their horses serve in the Mounted Branch
of Lothian and Borders Police. They were, of course, invited
when Ruth Skinner received her MBE for her work with Riding
and Carriage Driving for the Disabled in 2009.

Clydesdale steel sculpture in
Glasgow Business Park
Courtesy of Andy Scott Public Art

In 1997, a Clydesdale sculpture was unveiled in the City of Glasgow. Standing in the Glasgow Business Park, beside the M8 motorway, the sculpture, by Andy Scott, is made of welded galvanised steel bars varying from 6 to 20mm in diameter, and is 4 metres tall at the head. It can be interpreted at numerous levels: agriculture, the steel industry, heavy goods transport, and of course as a tribute to the Clydesdale breed. The horse, standing free of working harness, and its mane and tail dressed for exhibition, is a metaphor for the City which was once famed for industry and manufacturing, and is now, in the twenty first century, a city of art and culture.

The Kelpies on display at the
Falkirk Wheel
Courtesy of Andy Scott Public Art

Andy Scott has also used Clydesdales as models for The
Kelpies, 30 metre high sculptures of horses' heads, which will
form an integral part of a displacement lock boat system on the
Forth and Clyde Canal in Central Scotland. Each dip and rise
through a five metre span, displacing thousands of tons of water
to enable the boat lift mechanism, and will be in place from
2012. Models are on display at the Falkirk Wheel, and the
working sculptures promise to be a major landmark in the future.
Perhaps it is no accident that these colossal horses' heads should
have been the inspiration of Andy, himself a native of Falkirk
where the big horse Carnera was a local legend.

Heavenly Benedictine of Arclid, by Collessie Benedictine. Bred on the Isle of Man and owned by Little Big Ranch, Stromsund, Sweden
Courtesy of Little Big Ranch

2. Bloodlines and breeders:
history, studs, and stallion men

EARLY in the nineteenth century, farmers in the area known as Clydesdale in Lanarkshire set out to breed the type of horse required for more productive farming, and to meet the needs of Central Scotland's population growth and burgeoning industry.

The Statistical Account, written by the parish minister David Ure in 1793, has this version:

> 'Rutherglen fairs are famous for the finest draught horses in Europe. About a century ago an ancestor of the Duke of Hamilton brought six coach horses from Flanders and sent them to Strathaven – the castle then being habitable. They were all handsome black stallions. The surrounding farmers gladly bred from them and the cross with the Scotch horse procured a breed superior to either, which has improved with careful breeding.

> 'Great attention is paid to colour, softness and hardness of hair, length of body, breast and shoulders of their breeders. Every farm almost, has four or six mares. The colts are mostly sold at the fairs of Lanark or Carnwath. They excel in the plough, the cart or the wagon.'

It is also known that, between 1715 and 1720, John Paterson of Lochlyoch brought a Flemish stallion from England. This horse was said to have contributed greatly to the quality of the Lochlyoch mares which became famous during the late eighteenth century.

A nephew of Lochlyoch's tenant, by the name of Somerville of Lampits, bought a two year old filly in 1808. She became known as the 'Lampits mare' and bred the stallion named

Glancer, foaled in 1810, who was credited with being one of the best foundation sires, although he was known as 'Thompson's black horse' after his owner James Thompson of Germiston.

By 1850 a number of different blood lines had developed. Two breeders in particular had enormous influence, and from their establishments came the two stallions which produced the best breeding lines in Clydesdale history.

The first was Lawrence Drew, who was the Duke of Hamilton's factor, or land steward, at Merryton. The importance of good working horses to the tenants would be an influence on Drew's decision to establish a stud, together with the strong connection to the Hamilton family who were credited with the improvement of the Clydesdale breed.

There is no doubt that the fame of the Merryton Stud was largely due to the breeding of the great stallion Prince of Wales, whose direct descendants included Hiawatha, Apukwa and Fyvie Sensation.

The second was Davie Riddell, a dealer, who was responsible for shipping the finest Clydesdales to America, Australia, New Zealand and mainland Europe. He also owned Darnley, whose line boasted the famous stallions Sir Everard, Baron's Pride, Baron of Buchlyvie and Dunure Footprint.

In the late nineteenth century Clydesdale horse breeding was an important business, and huge amounts of effort, and money, were put in to selection to provide the best possible working horses. Good strong limbs were needed to carry the horse's great weight, and powerful muscles for pulling heavy loads. The large hoof is the shock absorber on a horse which had a higher step than the traditional farm cart horses, and which would be required to work long days on hard surfaces. A deep chest provided heart and lung room, vital for effort and stamina.

Continuous improvement was the aim, as the Clydesdale horse provided the agricultural and industrial power in our country for well over a century. By the early twentieth century,

Westforth Tara with twin foals, 1981
Tennant family collection

the following description of a good Clydesdale horse was published in the *Standard Cyclopedia of Modern Agriculture, Volume 3*:

'The Clydesdale is a very active horse. He is not bred for action, like the Hackney, but he must have action. But a Clydesdale judge uses the word with a difference. A Hackney judge using the word means a high-stepping movement, a Clydesdale judge means high lifting of the feet, not scuffling along, but the foot at every step must be lifted clean off the ground, and the inside of every shoe made plain to the man standing behind. Action for the Clydesdale judge also means 'close' movement. The forelegs must be planted well under the shoulders – not on the outside like the legs of a bulldog – and the legs must be plumb and, so to speak, hang straight from the shoulder to the fetlock joint. There must be no openness at the knees, and no inclination to knock the knees together. In like manner, the hind legs must be planted closely together with the points of the hocks turned inwards rather than outwards; the thighs must come well down to the hocks, and the shanks from the hock joint to the fetlock joint must be plumb and straight. 'Sickle' hocks are a very bad fault, as they lead to loss of leverage.

'A Clydesdale judge begins to estimate the merits of a horse by examining his feet. These must be open and round, like a mason's mallet. The hoof heads must be wide and springy, with no suspicion of hardness such as may lead to the formation of sidebone or ringbone. The pasterns must be long, and set at an angle of 45 degrees from the hoof head to the fetlock joint. Too long a pastern is very objectionable, but very seldom seen. A weakness to be guarded against is what is termed 'calf-knees,' that is the formation from the knee to the ground which begins with the knee being set back, giving the appearance of an angle which is delusive, because it is not the angle from the fetlock joint to the hoof head, which is a weakness and unsightly.

'A Clydesdale should have a nice open forehead, broad between the eyes, a flat (neither Roman-nosed nor 'dished') profile, a wide muzzle, large nostrils, a bright,

James Edgar Snr. bottlefeeding
Newfield Rose, 1968
Edgar family collection

clear, intelligent eye, a big ear, and a well-arched long neck springing out of an oblique shoulder with high withers. His back should be short, and his ribs well sprung from the backbone, like the hoops of a barrel. His quarters should be long, and his thighs well packed with muscle and sinew. He should have broad, clean, sharply developed hocks, and big knees, broad in front. The impression created by a thoroughly well-built typical Clydesdale is that of strength and activity, with a minimum of superfluous tissue. The idea is not grossness and bulk, but quality and weight.'

The Clydesdale Horse Society was founded in 1877, and a stud book was established, in order to legitimise pedigrees and clarify breeding lines. It is interesting that the system of district hiring stallions had begun as early as 1837, and many of these district societies held stallion shows in their own area. As the horse became more popular, and valuable, in the export market, the provenance of breeding became more important. That there has been joint ancestry between the Clydesdale and his English counterpart the Shire has never been in doubt, but as the Clydesdale developed and refined during the nineteenth century the establishment of demonstrably pure bloodlines was essential.

This move did not please everyone. Neither Drew nor Riddell attended the first council meeting, and in fact in 1883 they

Newfield Stud Card

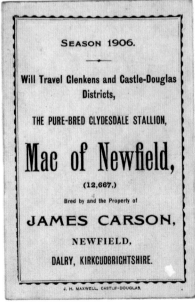

SEASON 1906.

Will Travel Glenkens and Castle-Douglas Districts,

THE PURE-BRED CLYDESDALE STALLION,

Mac of Newfield,

(12,667.)

Bred by and the Property of

JAMES CARSON,

NEWFIELD,

DALRY, KIRKCUDBRIGHTSHIRE.

J. H. MAXWELL, CASTLE-DOUGLAS.

PEDIGREE.

BRIDGEBANK MONOGRAM (21,175).

Black, white stripe on face, near fore pastern and hind legs white.

Foaled 15th April, 1924.

Breeder — Messrs G. & R. Findlater, Jerviswood Mains, Lanark.

Owner —
A. J. Marshall, Bridgebank, Stranraer.

Sire — Dunure Footprint (15,203).

Dam — Nellie of Cornhills (54,215) by Dandaleith Quest (19,082).

2d Dam — Nancy of Cornhills (47,738) by Duke of Brandon (17,861).

3d Dam — Rosie of Cornhills (31,109) by Copestone (10,723).

4d Dam — Rosie of Scoup (28,809) by Rosedale (8194).

5d Dam — Jess 2nd of Cornhills (28,808) by Charlie (14,625).

6d Dam ——— by Sir Walter Scott (797).

BRIDGEBANK MONOGRAM was winner of supreme champion at Lanark and West Linton Shows, 1924; 1st and champion at Stranraer and Wigtown Shows, and 2nd Ayr Show, 1925; and 3rd at Glasgow Stallion Show, 1927.

Dunure Footprint — Too well known to require comment.

Dandaleith Quest — Mr Pollock's noted horse, and winner of 1st at the Highland Society Show, 1921, and numerous other prizes. Sire, Dunure Footprint; dam, Queen Mary, by the famous Baron's Pride (9122); gr.-dam, by champion Marcellus (11,110).

Duke of Brandon — Sire, the 9500 guinea Baron of Buchlyvie, the sire of Dunure Footprint and the 5000 guinea Bonnie Buchlyvie; dam, Rosie of Brandon (23,799) by champion Hiawatha (10,067).

Copestone — Sire, the well-known Seaham Harbour stud horse, Primus (8897), by Prince of Wales (673); dam, Mona (11,519) by Old Times (579).

Rosedale, Charlie, and Sir Walter Scott — The most noted breeding horses of their time.

---

founded the 'Select Clydesdale Horse Society of Scotland' with the intention of registering any horse of the correct type, irrespective of breeding. This Society survived until 1888.

The Clydesdale Horse Society had friends in high places. The Prince of Wales was appointed Patron, and every Scottish peer in the House of Lords became a life governor. Such patronage was confirmed in 1891 when the Earl of Cawdor established two trophies to be awarded annually for the best of each sex. The Cawdor Cup is still the most sought after of Clydesdale awards, with the male championship judged at the Spring Stallion Show in March and the female at the Royal Highland Show in June each year.

The co-operation in the use of stallions was established through the district hiring service and ensured that local farmers from Orkney in the north to Galloway in the south had access to the very best bloodlines. Local horse breeding societies thrived, covering geographical areas which seem small today but were designed to allow for stallions, walked by their grooms, to travel from farm to farm over the course of a Spring and Summer season. Whether it was Castle Douglas and District, or the Orkney West Mainland Horse Breeding Society, top class horses were made available to farms to provide replacements for their working animals. An average farm of 250 acres would work 3 pairs of horses, always including mares for breeding.

Stud cards were produced for each stallion, either showing that the horse would 'travel the district of the above society' or 'will stand at home and meet mares by appointment'. Stud fees were set according to the quality or reputation of the stallion, and could be inflated as evidenced by the £40 set for Prince of Wales in 1876, or the 60 guineas at service and 60 guineas when the mare proved in foal for Dunure Footprint in 1918. By contrast, Dunure Measure, a son of Dunure Footprint, was standing in 1934 for a fee of £2 at service and £3 when the mare proved in foal, plus a Groom's fee of 2 shillings and 6 pence. Heavy Horse Breeding grants, from the government, provided subsidy to enable small farmers to use good stallions at reasonable cost.

The stallion man, or stallion leader, would be an experienced groom. Handling and caring for powerful stallions, and presenting them to mares, was a highly skilled job. The leader travelled alone with his horse, covering many miles in a week, bedding down at farms on the way where his charge was serving mares. If he was lucky he had a room in the farmhouse, otherwise he would be in the 'bothy', a loft accommodation above the stable.

William Crawford, a stud groom and stallion man for Albert Marshall at Bridgebank, Stranraer in the 1920s, walked stallions all over the south west of Scotland and over the border to England, travelling as far as Durham. Others went even further afield. One such was Jimmy Carson, a stallion man at Kilpatrick's Craigie Mains Stud who accompanied the very best horses to Canada, Australia, and New Zealand in the early 1900s. His wife Mary never left their tenement flat in Glasgow; she was a city girl and life alone in a farm cottage did not appeal. He obviously did come home occasionally, as they had eight children!

A veritable dynasty of Clydesdales was bred through the bloodlines of Darnley, his son Sir Everard, and Baron's Pride. Andrew Montgomery of Netherhall, Kirkcudbright, was probably the first breeder to bring the Clydesdale to prominence and

William Crawford exercising a stallion at Bridgebank, Stranraer, 1920s
Author's family collection

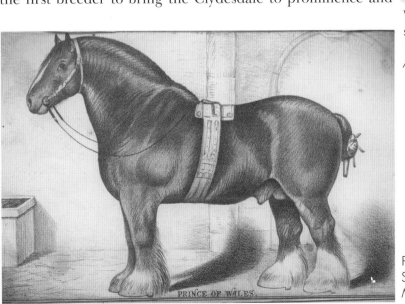

Prince of Wales, from the Merryton Sale Catalogue.
McMillan family collection.

MacGregor
Dumfries & Galloway Archives

promote them abroad. He bought MacGregor, a son of Darnley, as a yearling in 1879, and this horse went on to have considerable influence on prize winners, particularly in the United States. Andrew himself had travelled with his horses across the Atlantic, and some of his letters home, describing appalling weather conditions and the deaths of his horses, make harrowing reading. Enough reached North America, however, to ensure that buyers from the States and Canada made their way to Kirkcudbright to purchase the very best horses. At the height of the trade special trains left Kirkcudbright station early in the morning, loaded with Clydesdales to be shipped across the Atlantic from Liverpool

Docks. Local boys were recruited to lead the horses the two and a half miles to the station.

One such buyer was Hudson Allison, a wealthy Canadian from Montreal who had travelled to Scotland with his wife Bessie and their two children in 1912. A great lover of Clydesdales, he bought several from Montgomery at Banks before boarding the *Titanic* in Southampton in April. He and his wife, together with their 3 year old daughter, went down with the ship. The baby boy, also named Hudson, was taken to a lifeboat by his nurse and survived. One month after the funeral on 21st April in Montreal, the Clydesdales were delivered to Hudson's brother Percy.

The defining purchase, however, was in 1894 when Andrew's partner William bought Baron's Pride from R & J Findlay, Springhill, Baillieston. Foaled in 1890, he had been unsuccessful

Baron's Pride, a supremely successful breeding horse
The Clydesdale Horse Society

in the show ring, but William Montgomery saw his potential and bought him, together with one other, for £400. Apparently, after the deal was agreed, Findlay was told to keep the other horse.

Baron's Pride was a supremely successful breeding horse, much in demand as mares were sent to him from all over Britain. The Montgomerys managed him carefully, limiting him to no more than 90 to 100 mares a season. It was a privilege to get a nomination, but the proof of his impact on the Clydesdale breed is shown in the phenomenal success of his progeny. He sired eleven Cawdor Cup winners, and every winner of these championships, from 1905 onwards, has his blood in their pedigree. He died in 1912, and he is buried in a paddock to the south of Banks farmhouse. His groom was so moved by this great horse that he composed the following:

Strange was the phantom o'er the Banks of Kirkcudbright
As an arrow of death unknown to the Squire
Swiftly and silently pierced through the manger
Likewise through the heart of his great honoured sire.
A little lass playing did hear someone groaning
Then went to her father just close by her side.
'Oh Father' she said 'there is something the matter,
Oh come Father quick to your horse Barons Pride.'

Her father, the groom, was amazed for the moment,
Then boldly relented and went to her call.
But when he attained where the worthy was stabled
He found Baron dead with his back to the wall.
He thought at first he was just in a slumber
But after inspection proof could not hide;
But sadly he murmured these words to his daughter
'My dear, that's the end of the great Barons Pride.'

'The Baron is dead' were the words that were spoken,
The pride of the Empire has vanished at last,
But though he is gone we shall ever remember
The greatest of Clydesdales; the sire of the past.
Now Scotland is open for one to succeed him,
But friends we may search through the whole nation wide.
We might get a horse with an unbroken record
But never the type of the great Baron's Pride.

Since first the old Baron was known as a breeder,
His name has increased as king of the stud.
And during the years in the hands of his owners
His stock has revealed the worth of his blood.
But here is a question I am open to answer,
A question perhaps very strange to decide
Concerning the Baron of great reputation
Son of Sir Everard, the great Barons Pride.

The question is – Where can we find Baron's equal?
Whether a stranger or son of his own.
There is only one at Dunure Mains in Ayrshire,
Unbeaten for quality, substance and bone.
He stands well renowned, by the blood he's related,
And to his advantage there's youth on his side.
His son, The Dunure, is the horse of the future
If spared to the age of the great Barons Pride.

If ever a stallion on earth did his duty
Barons Pride proved himself as one of the best;
His sons and his daughters are famed for their beauty,
And all have been winners when put to the test.
He's known by all breeders of Clydesdales in Europe,
And lots of his gets have been shipped o'er the tide.
But now they are left with the last they can purchase,
Got by the genius, the great Baron's Pride.

His grandson I'm sure is the coming improver
If justice is granted wherever he goes.
At present he claims to be king of the nation
And proved himself champion all over the shows.
No judge can confute the remarks I have mentioned,
The Dunure shall conquer whatever betide.
He closely resembles the horse that is wanted
As king, and successor to old Barons Pride.

But though the old Baron is now dead and buried,
We cannot forget him for what he has done.
The worth of his blood has been proved to the country
By the price of Buchlyvie, his unbeaten son.
His death it has caused quite a public sensation,
Likewise is the talk of the whole countryside.
But now we must look to the coming successor
And mourn the loss of the great Barons Pride.

The enduring legend of Baron's Pride's son, The Baron of Buchlyvie, lives to this day due to the drama that unfolded over his ownership, and the incredible price paid for him at auction in Ayr in 1911. James Kilpatrick of Craigie Mains, Kilmarnock, bought him as a two year old for £700, and offered a half-share in him to William Dunlop of Dunure Mains, Ayr. The horse stood at Dunure after Dunlop had offered £2,000 for sole ownership, but the dispute arose over whether the £2,000 represented the whole value of the horse or just a half share. Court cases followed, in which the High Court decided in favour of Kilpatrick, but then Dunlop appealed successfully to the Court of Session. Kilpatrick in turn took his case to the House of Lords, which overturned the appeal and declared that the two men remained joint owners.

To say that relations between the two men made any form of working partnership impossible would have been an understatement. So it was decided that the horse should be put up for auction, and the proceeds shared by both claimants. In December 1911 the sale went ahead at Ayr Auction Market. A crowd of around 5,000 gathered to watch as the 12 year old horse was led in to the ring. The opening bid was £3,000, and this mounted rapidly to £7,000, at which point Dunlop apparently dropped out. Kilpatrick continued to bid, against a complete stranger, until the final price of £9,500 was knocked down to the unknown bidder. The auctioneer, James Craig, then shocked everyone by announcing that the winner was acting on behalf of William Dunlop. That the figure has gone down in the history books as a world record can readily be explained by the translation of this sum to current values, which in 2010 would be well over £700,000.

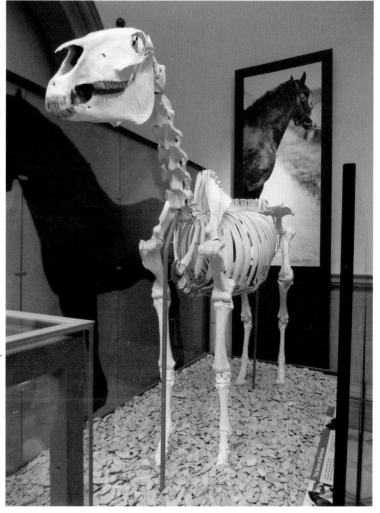

Baron of Buchlyvie skeleton in Kelvingrove Museum, Glasgow
Photo Nancy Anderson

It is said that Dunlop and Kilpatrick did not speak to each other for over twenty years.

Baron of Buchlyvie went home to Dunure, but two and a half years later he was kicked by a mare and had to be put down at the age of 14. He was buried in the rose garden at Dunure Mains, but later his remains were taken to Kelvingrove Museum in Glasgow where the skeleton is still on display.

Dunure Footprint, The Baron's most famous son, was born in 1908. By the time he died, aged 22, he had sired about 5,000 foals, due in no small part to his reputed serving of one mare every two hours, day and night, during the season. Supplementary feeding of stout, milk, and eggs kept him in condition, and his stud fees amounted to £15,000 over two seasons. His offspring won nearly every trophy in the country for thirteen years after his death, and his bloodlines are seen in pedigrees to this day.

Montgomery, Kilpatrick and Dunlop were three of the major studs in Scotland in the early part of the twentieth century. Kerr of Harviestoun, Dollar, and Marshall of Bridgebank, Stranraer, were only two of the other big names whose horses won major prizes and were coveted internationally.

A Clydesdale man who can't be forgotten is John G.S. Flett, a farmer and journalist from Nistaben, Harray, Orkney. As Secretary of the West Mainland Horse Breeding Society, he was instrumental in bringing superior Clydesdale blood to the Northern Isles in the 1920s and 30s, including three Cawdor Cup winners. He wrote for the local paper under the pen-name O.R. CADIAN, and it is under that name that the following poem was first published. The verses are still used today as a tribute and are a lyrical description of this most beautiful of horses.

Thudding hoof and flowing hair
Style and action sweet and fair
Bone and sinew well defined
Movement close, in front, behind.
Muscle strong, and frame well knit
Strength personified and fit.
Thus the Clydesdale – see him go
To the field, the stud, the show.

Noble eye, and handsome head,
Bold, intelligent, well bred;
Lovely neck, and shoulder laid
See how shapely he is made.
Proper back, and rib well sprung
Sound of limb, and sound of lung.
Powerful loin and quarter wide
Grace and majesty allied;
Basic horse, power-living force –
Equine King – The Clydesdale Horse.

Dunure Ernest taking a rest wth
groom Davie Heddle, Orkney
1931
Orkney Archives

The Picken family of Torrs, Kirkcudbright, were leading lights in the Clydesdale world for over three generations. The Torrs prefix was widely prized among breeders and by the time Jim Picken took over the farm in 1950 there were 76 horses there.

Jim was President of the Clydesdale Horse Society from 1978 to 1980, and his cousin David from Milton, Kirkcudbright, held the office from 1986 to 1988.

The Clark family of the Muirton Stud, near Crieff, have been breeding Clydesdales for more than 100 years, and have won the Cawdor Cup six times, most recently in 2010 with Muirton Sabre. The family also boasts an Honorary President of the

Littleward Esmerelda with the Carrick family in 1986. All the silverware, including the Cawdor Cup, was won in that year
Carrick family collection

Clydesdale Horse Society, Tom W. Clark, and the current President William Clark.

The late John Young established the Doura Stud of Clydesdales at West Doura, near Kilwinning in Ayrshire in the early 1950s, and became internationally famous in the years following his relocation to Girvan Mains in the 1960s. Stallions Doura Perfection, Doura Excelsior and Doura Masterstroke have left their names on the pedigree of countless Clydesdales on both sides of the Atlantic. The winning formula is carried on by his son Jim and granddaughter Charlotte, while his daughter Marion relocated to Canada in the 1980s to assist with the growing export business and has remained active as a judge and importer of Clydesdales in North America.

Few Clydesdale breeders of the last 100 years have built a reputation like Charles Carrick, from Thornhill, Stirlingshire. His expertise is legendary after over 60 years working with the breed, and a special dinner dance was held in his honour in April 2010 to celebrate his achievements which include winning the Foal Show five times. He has seven horses, but no stallions.

Ballochmorrie Mist, Cawdor Cup Winner, Royal Highland Show Kelso 1952
Clydesdale Stud Book Vol 74, 1953

He chooses stallions by bloodlines. 'You can breed tramps off toffs, but you can't breed toffs off tramps,' he avers. He looks for good bone, hairy legs, and close movement. 'The movement must be right,' he says. 'Half the horse is the hind legs.' Asked if any horses stand out in his memory over the years, he quotes Ballochmorrie Mist, the Cawdor Cup winner at the Royal Highland Show in 1952. Sired by Balgreen Final Command, she was a big, powerful mare and has been widely acknowledged as one of the greatest of the breed.

A picture of Charles and family with Littleward Esmerelda in 1986 is an indicator of his remarkable success in the show ring, in one year with just one horse.

Robert Hamilton founded the Dillars Stud near Lesmahagow in Lanarkshire over 20 years ago, and his horses have won the Cawdor Cup three times. Stock has been exported to Europe and North America, and it is a joy to drive past his fields, in the horse's native Clydesdale, and see them in their own landscape. Robert is also a past President of the Clydesdale Horse Society.

The Tennant family are a modern day dynasty in the world of Clydesdales. Tom, from Ettrick in the Scottish Borders, is the immediate past President of the Clydesdale Horse Society, and his father Peter remembers that Tom, aged 5, 'gret a' the way home' from the Stallion Show at the Kelvin Hall in 1964 when his gelding (also called Tom) was sold that day to Canada. Tom and Marjory's family are keeping up the tradition, with Gail winning the CHS Young Handler Trophy at the Royal Highland Show in 2007, and brother Andrew repeating the feat in 2010. Tom's brother, Peter, is also a breeder of note with his West Forth prefix, from Lanarkshire.

Tom Tennant aged 5, with his gelding 'Tom' at the Stallion Show in Kelvin Hall, Glasgow, 1964
Tennant family collection

The Tennant family and their Clydesdales at Carnwath Show 1982. The yearling fillies on the right are the 1981 twins
Tennant family collection

Gail Tennant, winner of the Royal Highland Show Young Handler's Competition 2007, with Clydesdale Horse Society President George Skinner
Tennant family collection

Gloom merchants will say 'it's only old men in Clydesdales these days.' If the roll call above hasn't convinced you, meet the Adamson family, John, Jacqueline, and their five children, from Glenside, Plean, Stirlingshire. John is a registered farrier, and was the youngest ever winner of the Cawdor Cup, aged 25, with Woodhouse Camilla in 1996, and was also the youngest judge of the Decorated Harness class at the Royal Highland Show in 1995. His grandfather, Peter Stewart, was a carter with Aitken's Brewery in Falkirk, and his mother, Mary Adamson, was a winner of the decorated harness class at the Royal Highland Show. Her family prefix, West Plean, has now been passed to John and Jacqueline's daughter Lyndsay, aged 12, who is successfully

John Adamson winning the
Cawdor Cup and Royal Highland
Show Championship in 1996 with
Woodhouse Camilla
Adamson family collection

Lauryn Adamson, aged 18
months, helps with the grooming
at Perth Show 2010
Adamson family collection

Lyndsay Adamson, aged 11, with her gelding West
Plean Bruno winning the National Stallion Show in
March 2010
Adamson family collection

showing all over Scotland. She won the gelding championship at the National Stallion Show two years in a row with two different horses, Kelvinhead Express in 2009 and West Plean Bruno, by Collessie Cut Above, in 2010.

Jacqueline is Secretary of the National Stallion show, and her grandfather, Jimmy Pettigrew, who farmed at Auchengree, Stepps, broke in and trained horses for Black & White Whisky. John and Jacqueline's horses are prize winners from Aberdeen to Great Yorkshire, and are much in demand. And if that family background isn't impressive enough, it looks like younger daughter Lauryn is starting early at the age of 18 months!

Thanks to dedicated breeders and horse lovers like these, the iconic heavy horse of Lanarkshire is thriving into a third century. A former Secretary of the Clydesdale Horse Society put it well:

'The infinite appeal of the Clydesdale horse is legendary. Not all of it is draped in antiquity or nostalgia.'
Stewart Gilmour, Secretary, The Clydesdale Horse Society, 1973

Jacqueline Adamson's grandfather, Jimmy Pettigrew, Auchengree, Stepps
Adamson family collection

Brewer's dray in Overgate, Dundee
*Dundee City Council, Central
Library, Local Studies*

Clydesdale with a fresh water butt.
Jubilee Celebrations, Queens Park,
1887
*Glasgow City Council Land and
Environmental Services*

3. City carters and town traders:
the Clydesdale at work in town and city

ALTHOUGH they are seen as an icon of our rural past, Clydesdales were as much a part of town dwellers' lives as they were of folk in the country. As well as the individual coal carts, milk carts, and rag and bone carts, there were the big stables of horses owned by the local city councils, haulage contractors, breweries and, of course, the Co-op.

In 1896, Glasgow Corporation had the biggest stable of Clydesdales in Britain. Over 370 of these horses followed the example of Glasgow's tenement dwellers and occupied a specially designed multi-storey stable in Bell Street. The four storeys had carts on the ground floor, a central courtyard, and the stables for the horses were on the upper floors. Ramps led up to them, there were cobbled floors to prevent slipping, and there were even specially designed fire escapes.

No slouches when it came to economy and efficiency, Glasgow Corporation's Cleansing Department were acknow-

Glasgow Cleansing Department Haghill Depot, 1918-1920, Carter John Thomson
Glasgow City Council Land and Environmental Services

Barr's Falkirk Factory 1901
Courtesy of A G Barr plc

ledged as the most efficient civic cleansing department in the world in 1911. Anything that could not be re-used or recycled filled in low grade swamp land which was fertilised with civic waste and used to grow hay, oats, wheat and turnips to feed the horses.

The horses were at the front line of removing domestic waste from people's homes, and they, along with their carters, were known by all the local people on their rounds. Not only were they fed and petted by passers by, they also became a 'dare' for the boys. If you couldn't, or wouldn't, run under the belly of a stationary horse, you didn't get in to the gang. Luckily for them, the Clydesdales lived up to their legendary gentleness.

The Aberdeen Shore Porters Society set up their Horse and Van Department in 1849. Carter's wages were 14 shillings a week. Only first class men were employed and many remained with the company for over 40 years. Good, heavy, sound horses were required and they went 'far and near' to procure them. Trace horses, owned by Wordie & Co, were provided to help with heavy loads from the Quay up Market Street, Guild Street and Commerce Street. A local animal lover donated a water trough

Mutter, Howie, railway carters for LMS
Aberdeen City Council, Library and Information Services, Local Studies

on Guild Street in 1858, which was finally removed in the early 1950s.

The Co-operative Wholesale Society, which traded in Scotland as S.C.W.S., was a major employer of horse transport through the first half of the twentieth century. In Glasgow alone they had a stable of 200 horses and 360 employees, and in 1922 the superintendent of carting, James C. Caldwell, was honoured at the City's Grosvenor Restaurant by the Clydesdale Horse Society for his services to the Clydesdale breed over the previous 30 years.

A.G. Barr & Co. began in Falkirk in 1830 as a cork cutting business, adding a soft drink business in 1875. By the turn of the century they were also trading from Glasgow, and all their deliveries were made by horse drawn lorries covering distances of up to ten miles out each day from their branches across the south of Scotland. The giant Carnera was certainly their best known horse, but others too had character aplenty. A driver salesman in Kirkcaldy in the 1930s remembers that his allocated horse, Bobby, knew the route when he started the job which was

Wordie's contractors' depot, West Street and Paisley Road, Glasgow
Royal Commission on the Ancient and Historical Monuments of Scotland; Licensor www.scran.ac.uk

just as well as the previous driver had refused to show him his round. On one occasion the horse was pulled in behind a Bread Society van to enable the salesman to visit a shop in Kirkcaldy High Street. He had only just started his sales pitch when the bread salesman came running back into the shop, shouting 'You'll have to pay for it!' He had left the back doors of his van open, and Bobby had helped himself to all the cream sponges and most of the cakes. His moustache all covered in cream, Bobby was quite content.

Barr's owned horses until 1959, but they were kept only for show purposes after 1952.

In 1842, William Wordie contracted with the Edinburgh and Glasgow Railway to collect and forward goods from the stations. That astute move led to the growth of one of the most important privately owned road transport companies in Britain, which remained in existence until after the railways were nationalised in 1948 and the road transport fleet became British Road Services. Wordie's horses were one of the most common sights in our towns and cities, even inspiring Dundee poet William McGonagall:

Twenty horses in a row
Every one of Wordie & Co.

Caledonian Goods Station,
Dundee, 1901
*Dundee City Council, Central
Library, Local Studies*

In the late nineteenth century the company bought over 300 horses a year, and by 1919 that had reached 576.

At their peak in the early twentieth century Wordie owned nearly three thousand horses. Clydesdales were the preferred breed, especially in Scotland, due to their brisk action and their ability to turn and back, although they had Shires, Percherons and Irish Draught horses too.

The line of trace horses at the bottom of West Nile Street in Glasgow, there to help pull heavy loads up the hill to High Street goods station, were familiar to all in the city centre. One story told is of a carter struggling to get his horse's nose bag on at dinner time, and the horse was tossing his head and being un-cooperative. A local worthy, who had perhaps enjoyed too much

Forth and Clyde Canal barge
drawn by a pair of Clydesdales,
1930
*Falkirk Museums; Licensor
www.scran.ac.uk*

of a liquid lunch, was heard to call out, 'Hey mister! You'll no get that big horse intae that wee bag!'

The contractor's depot, built for them and designed by architect William Tennant, was a noted landmark on the corner of West Street and Paisley Road West. Three storeys high, with a central courtyard, it contained 151 stalls, 12 loose boxes, and space for the horse lorries. The lorries were on the ground floor, with the stables on the first floor and the loft for storing hay and grain for horse feed.

In Dundee Wordie horses were used heavily by the jute mills, and for shunting railway wagons; their stables in Dock Street had 126 horses in 1928. In Edinburgh they pulled brewery lorries.

The towns along the Forth and Clyde Canal were well served in the nineteenth and early twentieth century by both freight and passenger traffic. The fly-boats, hauled by relays of horses, were popular for high speed travel between Glasgow and Falkirk until the railways offered competition in the mid-1800s. By the early twentieth century up to seventy percent of haulage on the canal was provided by steam lighters, known as 'puffers' because of the sound from the engine exhausts. Coal, stone, timber and manure were the most usual cargoes, and horses were still in use until World War II. One user was Robinson Dunn the timber merchants, who used horse drawn barges to draw timber to and from their sawmill at Temple. Horses could pull a load of 50 tons on the canal, but only 2 tons on a good road, and the canals were a highly efficient means of transporting heavy or bulky goods. One lady is quoted as saying, 'I remember the Clydesdale horses. . . It was quite a nice sight to see and the canal bank was beautiful with wild roses and hawthorn.'

The canal stables at Glasgow Bridge, near Kirkintilloch, which housed the horses and the bridge-keeper, is now converted into a restaurant.

Horses were widely used in most towns by cleansing departments and parks. But as the tractor and motorised lorry became more readily available, with the advantage of speed, and the difficulty of finding experienced horsemen, horses were gradually phased out after the end of World War II. In Kirkintilloch in 1945 it was proposed that the last remaining horse be disposed of, as there was not enough work to justify keeping it. The following poem appeared in the local paper, the *Kirkintilloch Herald*:

THE AULD HORSE
REPLIES TAE THE COUNCIL

Ye honest folk who rule the toon,
It seems you're goin' to shoot me doon,
Since I'm no fit tae get aroon',
An' serve democracy;
I realize, wi' my horse sense,
The plan is wise – wid save expense,
But using kindness as pretence
Is damned hypocrisy!

For sixteen years I served you weel,
Till noo nae carts I'm fit to wheel,
On strength of service I appeal
Afore you shoot;
This wee concession I wid ask,
Since I'm no fit tae dae a task,
Jist in a grass park let me bask
An' roam aboot!

If ye canna get me tae a farm,
Noo Simmer days are comin warm,
Lyin' oot wid dae nae harm
Tae such as me;
Ye ken I'm no just like yoursel',
Wi' hope o' Heaven and fear o' Hell
So on this planet let me dwell
Until I dee.

I wrocht for you when at my best,
Don't treat me as you wid a pest,
So whit aboot a Simmer's rest,
By way o' pension?
It's no tae wisdom I'm appealin',
But tae yer boasted human feelin',
That you are usin' for concealin'
Your real intention.

Fallen horse at Dundee Harbour Police Station in the early 1900s
Dundee City Council, Central Library, Local Studies

Officials and councillors hardened their hearts and the horse was destroyed.

Horse shoe-ers, or blacksmiths, were much in demand for the horses. Depending on the road surfaces, shoes could last for as little as two weeks, and never longer than six. Wordie's at West Street had four blacksmiths working from 6am to 4pm with two half hour breaks on weekdays, and from 6am to 9am on Saturdays. Each man shod six horses in a full day, and made shoes in the afternoon at three pairs an hour, each pair being either front or back. In 1939 the pay was 3 pounds 9 shillings for a 48 hour week.

Every town had at least one blacksmith's shop. Ian Wade started as an apprentice in 1944 at the age of 14, for a wage of 15 shillings and 6 pence for a 48 hour week at the smiddy in

Barrhead. After the war his wage was 5 pounds a week, and shoeing cost 28 shillings for a farm horse which might be shod every three months, and 30 shillings for a contractor's horse every four to five weeks. Big customers at the blacksmith's in Love Street, Paisley, were the Burgh Cleansing Department and the Co-op.

Shoeing for a town horse was specialised. Toe pieces were welded on, and one inch heels gave grip. Cogs or studs were added in winter to help in frosty conditions, and these were taken out each night to prevent the horse injuring itself while lying down in the stall.

Until the early 1980s, a popular sight in Glasgow City Centre was a team of James Buchanan & Company's Clydesdale 'Black & White' geldings pulling a dray loaded with whisky to deliver to local establishments. Stabled in Warroch Street, right by the River Clyde just off the Broomielaw, they continued to work until the increase of motorways and new traffic systems reduced the routes they could use. Bobby Woods, the head carter, told of his horse Chester stealing a woman's shopping bag when he was stopped at traffic lights, and making off down the Broomielaw with it. Doubtless he expected it to contain carrots, sugar, or mints!

It was a long hard day for a carter. Mostly they had to be at the stables by 6am, in order to feed, water, muck out and groom their horses before harnessing them and yoking them to the lorries. Station horses would be led to the railway yard where the lorries were kept, others were yoked at the stable yard. Other than a 'piece-break' at dinner time, when the horses would be given their feeds in a nose-bag, they worked until five without stopping. Then they had to get back to the stables and do everything in reverse, taking off the harness, grooming and drying off their horses before feeding them and bedding them down for the night. Many of the horses were so well accustomed to their routine that, after a drink at the yard trough on their return, they made their own way up the ramp to the stables and into their own stall to wait to be unharnessed. Feed was usually bruised oats, chop (chopped hay) and hay. Sometimes a little

Black & White Whisky
Clydesdales deliver in
Glasgow streets
*Courtesy of Diageo
Brands B.V.*

Black & White Clydesdales at their stables in Warroch Street, Glasgow
Courtesy of Diageo Brands B.V.

treacle might be added, or a few sliced turnips.

Each man was responsible for cleaning his own harness, and many took items home to clean them. They took turns at looking after the horses at weekends and some spent that time giving their harness extra care. For most the turnout of their horse, harness and wagon was a matter of great pride and the bond they forged with their equine partner was one of mutual trust and affection.

In May 1911, 20 Clydesdale horses made history as they hauled the world's largest anchor from Noah Hingley & Sons, in Netherton, West Midlands to Dudley Railway Station two miles away. Destined for Harland & Wolff in Belfast, the 18ft 6in long, 10ft 9in wide, 15ton 16cwt centre anchor was ordered for the new transatlantic liner *Titanic*.

Transportation for the anchor was sub-contracted by LNWR (London and North Western Railways) to the Midlands haulage company W.A. Ree. They sent a large dray and eight of their Clydesdale horses, which were a common sight on the waterways, canals and roads of the area. These horses, each with a pulling

Tennents Breweries Unicorn Hitch
at the Royal Highland Show 1989
Scotsman Publications Ltd

Milkman Ronnie O'Connor, St.
Cuthberts Co-op Dairy, Edinburgh,
out at sunrise in 1984
Scotsman Publications Ltd

Roddy the railway horse
demonstrating shunting
Courtesy of Jamie Quinn

Titanic anchor forged at
N. Hingley & Sons,
Netherton, being pulled
through the streets to
Dudley Railway Station
by twenty Clydesdale
horses
*Dudley Archives & Local
History Service: Ref. P/
91 Donated by Mr.
A.R.Guy*

strength of up to two tons, were connected to the cart after the anchor had been lowered onto it. As there were challenging hills en route, Hingley works decided to attach six of their own horses to the Ree horses to help take the strain on inclines and cobbles. And from the LNWR terminal, another six horses were sent to assist if required. They were placed at the head of the team and returned to their depot as part of the magnificent procession of twenty Clydesdales. Hundreds of townsfolk lined the two mile route to see the world's largest anchor on its way to Fleetwood, from where it would cross the Irish Sea to the Belfast shipyards of Harland & Wolff and be fitted aboard the *Titanic*.

Woolmet Coalworks horse going to Leith Links Show
Midlothian Council Library Services, Local Studies

Alfie Work harrowing with horses
at Quoymoan, Orkney
Orkney Archives

4. Field and forest:
the Clydesdale at work on the land

And oh the rapture, when, one furrow done,
They marched broad-breasted to the sinking sun!
The light flowed off their glossy sides in flakes;
The furrows rolled behind like struggling snakes.

From 'Horses' by Edwin Muir

CLYDESDALE horsemen started young. Bob Donnachie first worked Clydesdales in 1945 at the age of 12, at Barns of Claverhouse near Dundee. When he returned from National Service in 1953, he went to Whitfield to life in a bothy, with two working pairs and show horses. That farm had Percherons working alongside the Clydesdales. 'Farmers bought working horses according to their purses,' says Bob. When he went to Balruddary, near Invergowrie in 1960, he was put in charge of two working pairs and a 'staig' or unbroken colt. His basic weekly wage then was 9 pounds a week, with 1 pound extra for the second pair plus another 1 pound for breaking in the young horse. His days started at 5.30 am, watering the horses before their first feed and his breakfast.

Bill Todd was even younger. At the age of 10 he was riding the Clydesdales from Brockloch Farm, New Cumnock, to Benson Smiddy on Saturdays. He was given the job of walking the furrow horse up and down the burn to clean its legs after a day at the plough.

Jim Irving started at Parkhouse Farm, Canonbie in 1945 at the age of 14. A Buccleuch Estates tenancy, Parkhouse had seven horses in 1945, with two full time horsemen. The day started at 6 am with the first watering and feed. At 7 the horses were harnessed, ready for the day's work. At 12 noon there was a one hour break, when the horses were taken back to the stable,

Andrew Elphinstone, Grieve at Broomhill Farm, on the right of his line-up of Clydesdales
Courtesy of Mrs Lorraine Clark

watered and fed, and the men went home for their dinner. At 1 they were back at work until 6 pm. Pay was 2 pounds 10 shillings a week for $5\frac{1}{2}$ days, as Saturday mornings were routinely worked. In summer, with the extra hours required for hay and harvest, six Saturday afternoons had to be worked before overtime was paid. The horsemen took turns to look after the horses on a Sunday.

Looking after your horses was a priority. They were groomed first thing, then again following a drink at the yard water trough on the way back to the stables. After that grooming, cleaning the horse after a hard day's work, they were taken back to the water trough for another drink before the last feed of the day and bedding down for the night.

Farm stables were stalls, with horses tied to the heavy fixed trough by a rope and 'sinker', which allowed enough freedom of movement for the horse to lie down but prevented their legs tangling in a loose tether. Feed was usually crushed oats, sometimes supplemented by cut turnips, and hay fed in the hay rack alongside the trough. Most were bedded on straw, as sawdust manure was of limited use on the farm.

Piece break during a ploughing match at Windygates, Haughhouse, Leven, 1931
National Museums Scotland, Scottish Life Archive

Unlike urban horses farm Clydesdales went out to grass in summer, except when they were in heavy work when they would be stabled.

On farms with more than one horseman there was a very strict hierarchy. The senior man, as the first horseman or first ploughman, always led the others out to work in the mornings. He and his horses were first, and woe betide any worker who failed to give him his place. There was great pride in being a horseman and in the condition of the horses and the quality of the work.

One man with a pair of horses could plough a good acreage every day, covering a distance of up to 12 miles. And there was no disguising poor work. Anyone could see if the furrows were crooked or the headland uneven. Many farms had fields named according to the ploughing process – the 'AeFur' meaning that

Donald Smith, one of the last in Scotland to farm entirely with horses, ploughing at Lowes, Corsock, in the 1970s
Photo Drew Taylor

it could only be ploughed in one direction, or the 'ForeDark' if it could be worked in one day.

Ploughing matches were a great test of skill and were the keenly contested highlight of the year. Horse ploughing matches are still held today, giving us a chance to watch the age old process of man, horse and nature working together.

Four horse grubbing rig at
Twynholm, Kirkcudbright
Dumfries & Galloway Archives

WALKING BEHIND HORSES

Walking behind horses brought a kind of peace.
Even the hissing ploughshare and turning furrow,
The rip of hard roots and the lapwings' call
Made more of an internal, inward quiet.
The straining beasts stepped on, hooves clicked,
The draught chains jingles on the swingle trees,
And how again is to be found that calm
That has vanished now even from empty fields
Where no man's fist holds reins behind a team?

William Neil

Potato planting at Wolfstar Farm,
Pencaitland, 1940s
*National Museums Scotland,
Scottish Life Archive*

Jimmy Copland cutting hay at
Holehouse Farm, Durisdeer, 1930s
Courtesy of Mrs Morag Murray

Murray Smith turning hay at
Lowes, Corsock, late 1960s
Smith family collection

If there is romance and nostalgia in the memories of a
ploughman and his horses, there is very little in the task which
preceded it in the farming year – muck spreading. The dung
from the byres, cattle sheds and stables was forked and barrowed
either to a midden or dung heap, or, in some cases, forked direct
onto the cart from the byre door. For those in any doubt, cattle
dung is heavy!

The horse stood patiently while the cart was loaded by fork
(or graipe, as the four pronged dung fork was called). Although
John Dodd, who still farms entirely with horses at Sillywrea in
Northumberland, recalls one occasion when he was mucking
out the byre and one of the cows was lying down, so far back in
her stall that he couldn't get the muck from behind her. 'Get
up!' he said. Unfortunately his horse Winston took the instruc-
tion to heart and set off for the field without him.

Archie Steel on top of a hayrick at South Allerton Farm, Jackton, 1925. The horse was called Blyth and, left to right, Agnes Steel, Jimmy Willing, Tam Weir, Matthew Steel, and 'the maid'
Steel family collection

The loaded cart was taken out to the field and the muck dumped in heaps. On some farms it was spread from the cart, saving the return on foot to spread and fertilise the field evenly. An experienced horseman could move anything up to twenty cartloads a day, depending on the distance from the yard to the field. But at the end of the day, he smelled anything but sweet! A houseproud wife often made her man strip off outside the back door when he'd been spreading dung.

Ploughed fields were grubbed and harrowed to get them ready for sowing, usually in early Spring. The horse-drawn seed drill replaced hand sowing, where the worker carried a seed box or bag on his shoulders and spread the corn to either side with regular sweeps of his arms to either side. Two horses could sow an acre an hour, but the horseman had to keep his mind on the job. Keeping the seed flowing freely and evenly, and making sure that ground was neither sown twice or missed, were vital.

Bill Harris on the binder, with William Taylor in centre and Jimmy Harris with children Jimmy and Jane, at Cairnpark Farm, Fintry in the 1920s
Courtesy of Pamela Duncan

Failure at either would show up, and damage a reputation, as soon as the growth appeared.

Hay time was one of the most important spots on the farming calendar. The window of time between June and July was crucial, as hay was essential winter feed for all the livestock, and a good hay crop set the farm right for the year. A two horse mower, with the horseman sitting on a sprung seat above the cutting blades, would start in the early morning to get the maximum cut and take advantage of the sun's warmth and drying power on the cut swathes. This would be followed by the hay-turner, drawn by a single horse and designed to flip each swathe over to dry the underside.

When the hay was dry, the Tumblin' Tam, or hay sweep, was used to gather the swathes together into heaps. So called because of the somersault action of the spikes, they were hard work but

Farm workers in front of grain
stacks, Inverdovat Farm, Newport
on Tay, 1910
*National Museums Scotland,
Scottish Life Archive*

useful when labour was scarce as they made the job of getting the hay in a bit quicker. The heaps were then forked into ricks about eight to ten feet tall, weighed down by ropes pegged in to the foot of each one, and these were carted back to the stack yard by a single horse towing a rick lifter, or low loading trailer, which was backed under the hay rick at an angle. The hay was then positioned on the trailer to ensure that it could be safely carted along tracks and through gates back to the yard, where it was built into giant stacks or loaded into the hay shed and hay lofts ready for the winter. Everyone on the farm helped, wives and children too.

Neill Ross was a boy at the Bennan, near Moniaive, where they had three horses, Charlie, Major and Betsy.

'I can remember the feeling of being on top of the world

Gathering turnips for winter feed, Scottish Borders
The Robert D. Clapperton Photographic Trust

when I was set astride the back of one of them after a day at the hayfield, with either my Dad or Uncle Tom behind me. I can remember even my mother behind me and she was wearing trousers! It was a great feeling with the slow rhythmic plod and the rattle of the harness chains – magic!'

September was traditionally harvest time. Summer sun had ripened and swelled the grain, and now it was all hands to work to get the crop safely in before the wet weather came. Depending on the land and the crop, the reaper-binder would be drawn by two or three horses. The big wooden paddles revolved and pushed the corn against the cutter blades, dropping the cut crop onto canvas belts that propelled it to the separator where it was formed into sheaves and knotted with twine. Workers

January 1, 1942.   *THE SCOTTISH FARMER*   19

Alexr. Jack & Sons, Ltd., Maybole

(Established 1835)

Agricultural Implement Manufacturers   **Home Timber Merchants**

JACK'S *FAMOUS*

CARTS. TRACTOR CARTS. LORRIES. TIMBER WAGONS. RICKLIFTERS. BARROWS AND TROLLIES OF EVERY DESCRIPTION.

∗

ALL fitted with DUNLOP Pneumatic Wheel Equipment.

∗

The Most Progressive Innovation of Modern Times.

THE "AJAX" LIME AND BASIC SLAG DISTRIBUTOR.

SIMPLEST MACHINE ON THE MARKET.

NEW IMPLEMENTS

Combined Three Drill Plow, Manure Distributor and Dibbler. Awarded Silver Medal at Alloa Highland Show, 1937, and at Ayr Show, 1938.

Three Drill Cultivator with Shafts for One Horse. Awarded Silver Medals at Ayr Show, 1937, and Belfast Show, 1938.

THE WORLD'S BEST POTATO DIGGER

JACK'S "CALEDONIAN"

THE ORIGINAL AND STILL THE BEST.

MAKERS OF

THE "PERFECT" DOUBLE DRILL PLOW & MANURE DISTRIBUTOR. THE "IMPERIAL" MANURE DISTRIBUTOR. THE "EMPIRE" MOWER & REAPER. HAY RAKES. HAY COLLECTORS. RICKLIFTERS. TURNIP SOWERS. DISC DRILL SCARIFIERS. HARROWS. HUNTER HOES. FOOD COOLERS. STRAW BARROWS. &c.

The Scottish Farmers' Plow—The "DUX"

Quality Tells.
Use only Genuine "DUX" Fittings and get satisfaction

The Sole Importers of the " Dux "

ALEXR JACK & SONS, LTD.

MAYBOLE. *Telephone—Maybole* 2188

∗

Depot at 20 GRAHAM SQUARE, GLASGOW, E. *Telephone—Bridgeton* 713

Farm implements advertisement in the *Scottish Farmer*
The Scottish Farmer Annual

Watering place on the way home
Aberdeen City Council, Library and Information Services, Local Studies

walked along behind, gathering the sheaves into stooks of eight or ten sheaves, sloping inwards so that any rain would run off. When the stooks had dried, they were carted in to the stack yard to wait for 'the big mill' – the threshing machine that separated the corn from the straw. Big mill day could be any time over the winter, and helpers came from all over the area.

Rev. Sandy Gunn remembers September 1950:

'I was nervous. This was the last year that Roy, the veteran Clydesdale who had escaped war service, would be pulling the cart into the stack yard, and I had been promised a chance to build a load for the leading. What a thrill! No longer the backbreaking task of forking up the sheaves, but the privilege of arranging them in order on the cart. If I succeeded in this, perhaps next year I might be allowed to build a stack: not the top, of course, for it required skill, hard earned by years of experience, to taper this to a central point, but nevertheless a stack, *my* stack!

'Now the test! Round the stack yard was a drain. . . Would the load reach the stack yard, or would there be the humiliation of the load slipping as it swayed and lurched over the drain and on to the cobbles? It seemed as if Roy knew. Slowly and sedately he allowed me to square the cart at right angles to the drain, and then, with a strong pull, it was over.

'Success. I could therefore hold my head high on the day the mill came to the farm. All the men from around turned up to help. Forking, cutting the twine, each man had a job. No money was exchanged – everyone knew and helped everyone else. The odd bag of tatties mysteriously appearing during the winter months would help. Last year I was just a boy, carrying the water from the well, bringing out the broth, and at tea-time, the scones dripping with raspberry jam. Now I had built my load. I was a man.'

The bond men had with their horses was deep. This ballad, by George Corrigall from Orkney, may be sentimental but it resonates with all but the hardest hearted.

It wasn't only the arrival of the grey 'Fergie' tractor that contributed to the reduction of horses on our farms. Many good horses were lost to grass sickness, or grass-ill as it was known in

Dress harness in Huntly,
Aberdeenshire, 1930s
Aberdeen City Council, Library and Information Services, Local Studies

PRINCIE AND JEAN

I'll sing you a song o' a canty auld body,
A kenspeckle figure wis auld Wattie Broon,
A trustworthy hand at the Mains o' Drumcloddie
Sin' the day he began tae work there as a loon.
An' syne there as Baillie he proved himself canny,
His work conscientious, particular an' clean,
Till ae day his maister said 'Wattie, ma mannie,
Ye'll tak' the third pair, they're ca'd Princie and Jean.'

And in a' bonnie Scotland there wasna a human
So happy as Wattie wi' his dandy pair.
He soon held his ain wi' the rest as a plooman,
And, oh, was he prood o' his gelding and mare!
A grand pair o' blacks, no' their like in a hunner,
Wi' coats o' a rich glossy ebony sheen,
An' at plooin' matches for years worthy winner
For grooming, was Wattie, wi' Princie and Jean.

So Wattie aye bided, content wi' his duties,
But life's fu' o' changes, as a'body kens,
Decrepit auld age claimed the baith o' his beauties,
And tractors began tae appear at the Mains.
A steerin' wheel Wattie jist wadna be grippin',
He wrocht on as orra man – didna compleen,
But a'body noticed puir Wattie was slippin'
Doonhill, he was pinin' for Princie and Jean.

And noo he's awa', a' his trauchles are ended,
A God-fearin' body that aye did his best,
His life was a sermon, the mourners a' kent it
On Tuesday last week when we laid him to rest.
And we a' had a thocht, though we didna divulge it,
As wi' hankies we dabbit the tears fae oor een,
That if He wha was born in a manger so wills it,
They'll be waitin' for Wattie – his Princie and Jean!

George Corrigall

the North of England, a mysterious wasting disease that had first appeared in a camp of Army horses in Angus in 1908. Suggested causes have been many, from a fungus on the grass, or a form of botulism, but the result was, in most cases, a cruel and inevitable death. John Dodd tells of one farmer near Stamfordham in Northumberland who lost three different pairs of horses in one year before he got his hay in. The cost in heartbreak was considerable; in economic terms it was devastating. With nursing and dedicated care, a chronic case can be brought through to survival, although they are never wholly fit again. For a working farmer, whose horses were the power on the land, the spread of grass sickness was a disaster for which there was neither prevention nor cure.

The National Coal Board had fifteen farms covering some six thousand acres in Northumberland, and at one time had fifty Clydesdales working on them. Alan Reed used to go tattie picking while he was at school and got the chance to drive a horse. When he left school in 1950, Grange Farm was working three pairs of horses and a single, and Alan got the single one. The farms were run by the Coal Board after the land was bought for mining and in their heyday the NCB horses were shown successfully from the Highland Show in Scotland to the

Clydesdale with grass sickness
Courtesy of Jenny Henderson

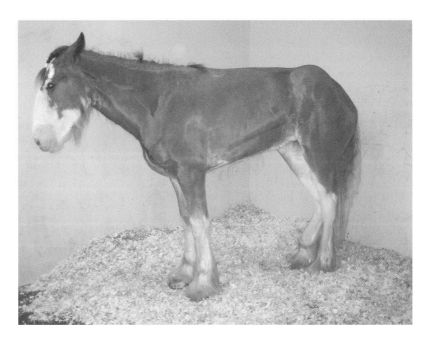

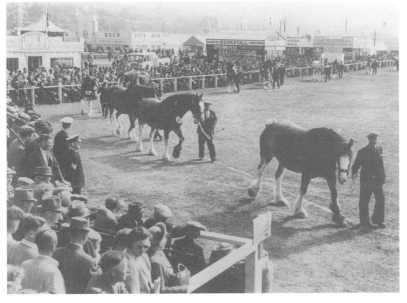

Midlands. The land was originally bought to avoid claims for subsidence caused by mining operations, but the farms became profitable as demand for food grew. In the 1930s their dairy herds supplied much of the local milk around Ashington. But by the time Alan came back from National Service the horses were on their way out, and when the land was turned over to Alcan in the 1950s, the farms were broken up and the horses

National Coal Board Clydesdales in a 4 horse hitch
Courtesy of Alan Reed

National Coal Board Clydesdales at the Royal Highland Show, Dundee, 1949
Courtesy of Alan Reed

were shipped live, in open trucks, from Ashington Station to Antwerp in Belgium for slaughter. From showpiece to super-fluous, the Clydesdale was at the mercy of changing priorities. Galloway poet Allan Wallace sees the work of horses like these as a debt that can never be repaid.

> They hae plou'ed frae early morn
> Worthy they the bite o' corn,
> Sweat it daes the horse adorn
> Through labour sair.
> But they are nae doot tae man
> A faithful pair.
>
> Lang the years horse toiled the lan',
> Some seen kind, some cruel han'
> That on them did render man
> 'Twas times unjust.
> And tae think that man's best frien'
> His gut wud bust.
>
> Efter day whun worked their best
> They are worthy o' their rest.
> A' the toil they did invest
> And effort made;
> Never could man see this debt
> Tae horse repaid.

The last of Jock O'Brough's Clydesdales coming off the boat from Westray at Kirkwall Pier, 1968
Orkney Archives

William Templeton working in woods near Closeburn, Dumfriesshire around 1950
Courtesy of Isobel Henkelman

Horses were important in forestry management too. Big estates like Buccleuch, and even smaller landowners who had significant areas of woodland, kept horses purely for wood work. A horse has the capability of access where machinery fails, and can handle steep slopes and narrow tracks. But it's hard work, and requires a great deal of skill.

Sheila Murray's father Robbie Henry was a woodsman with Buccleuch Estates until his death in 1973. He looked after his own horse, which was stabled near their home outside Canonbie. His day began at 7.15 and ended at 5.15, with a dinner break when the horse got home for a feed. The grain and hay was supplied by the Estate. But Robbie watered, fed, groomed and

Robbie Henry, Buccleuch Estates
Woodsman at Canonbie, 1960
Courtesy of Sheila Murray

mucked out at both ends of the day, and never took a holiday because the horse needed looking after. Sheila remembers that one of the horses, Prince, always stopped at the house gate for a piece of bread on his way to a day pulling out cut trees.

It was wet, mucky and dangerous work. It takes a real horseman to hold and manage a horse while he attaches the chains to a single log, and to make sure that it doesn't roll, or catch on a tree stump, or break the chain. And picking your way down a steep wood track with a loaded wood cart is no picnic.

One of the hardest jobs for a horse would be carting stone from the quarries that provided building materials. Some, like granite and sandstone, were highly prized and even shipped abroad. But for the horses that pulled the heavy loads there was little glamour. Dust and sweat made for little comfort, and only the care and kindness the lucky ones were shown by the carters made their lives bearable, as this little poem describes.

THE QUARRY HORSE

Ye muckle, pouerfu', handsome horse
O the michty Clydesdale breed,
Rosettes which pedigree endorse
Aince graced yer noble heid.

A fine braw sicht ye must hae been
When yokit tae the plou,
As harness shone and buckles gleam,
A show horse, through an' through.

But noo ye staun wi' heid held low,
A' clarty an forlorn.
Nae buckles gleam, nae leathers glow,
Yer harness dull an' worn.

For ye are noo a Quarry horse,
A' happit owre wi stour.
Does he wha selt ye, wi' remorse
Regret that evil 'our?

Tae condemn ye, sic a noble beast
Tae a life o' toil an' scorn;
Jist ae guid thing, yer daily feast
O' locust pods an' corn.

Yer sinews tense, yer muscles po'er,
On the rails the wheels dae ring
As ye pu the bogie fu' o' stour
Up owre the stourie bing. . .

Robert M Banks

Quarry horse at Kirkpatrick Fleming sandstone quarry
Dumfries & Galloway Archives

Carting peat at Stromness, Orkney
Orkney Archives

Clydesdales weren't only used by whisky distillers to deliver casks in cities. In the early part of the twentieth century horse power was a hugely important part of the distilling process. From carting the cut peat to the transport of grain and barrels, teams of horses were employed at distilleries like the Glenlivet at Minmore Farm. It was only in 1960 that the horse and cart at the Knockdhu Distillery was replaced by a tractor.

The countryside's reliance on horses was the driving force behind other local businesses. Every village had a blacksmith's, and sometimes a 'smiddy' could be found out in the countryside, serving far flung farming communities. On some farms the working horses were unshod, and the farmer would trim their feet. Others, though, had their horses trimmed and shod regularly. The smith made all the shoes and sometimes shod up to 30 horses a day, as well as doing local machinery and ironwork. There was usually a long queue at the blacksmith's on a wet day, when farm tasks were held up due to the weather. Even before there were formal qualifications in farriery, the blacksmith's was a trade to be proud of. The late Edward Martin, the third and last generation of farriers in Closeburn, Dumfries-

Saddler's mark from draught horse saddle, early twentieth century
Courtesy of Lewis Currie; Photo Nancy Anderson

Blacksmith William Cluckie at Sanquhar Smiddy. The cast iron horse figure above the entrance was based on Craigie Dalpeddar, the champion stallion born in 1932 who was bred at nearby Dalpeddar Farm and ran in the field behind the smiddy after he was weaned
Courtesy of Mrs Irene Riddall

shire, remembered, as a teenager, asking his father for a wage, now that he was working. His father put down his hammer and replied 'What do you want a wage for? You're being given a trade.'

Saddlers were another common business, usually in the small towns. Making harness was, and is, a great skill, and was a trade that was highly valued. Working harness was in constant need of repair, as worn harness can rub and injure the horse, and can even be dangerous if it breaks while in use. The saddler's workshop was a fascinating place, with pieces of leather, felt, string and that wonderful smell of leather and horses, and the saddler bent over his bench.

For some in the most rural communities, the Clydesdale also brought the grocer's shop. Mobile shops were pulled by horses before the motor van, and brought essentials to the outlying farms and crofts.

(below) Robertson's Grocery Van, Hope, Orkney. 1920
Orkney Archives

Commandeering horses at Newton Stewart in 1914
Whithorn Photographic Group Licensor www.scran.ac.uk

5: The Front and the Farm:
the Clydesdale in war

We didn't know much about it.
We thought they'd all come back
But off they all were taken
White and brown and black;
Cart and cab and carriage,
Wagon and break and dray,
Went out at the call of duty
And we watched them go away.
All of their grieving owners
Led them along the lane
Down the hill to the station,
And saw them off by train.

RSPCA 'In Aid of Funds for Wounded Horses' 1916

WHILE some of the Clydesdale's ancestors, the Flemish stallions imported in the eighteenth century to Lanarkshire, were undoubtedly of the type ridden by the knights of old and romantically described as war horses, it was in the twentieth century that our native heavy horse was called upon to serve his country in a war of unimaginable ferocity and duration.

On November 11th each year, Armistice Day, we remember the enormous sacrifice of the men and women who fell in the Great War and subsequent conflicts. And rightly so. But over a quarter of a million horses were lost by the British on the Western Front in World War I, and only about 60,000 of these were destroyed by enemy fire. Most died due to the appalling weather and unspeakable conditions. Not all were Clydesdales, of course, or even heavy draught horses. But all were conscripted from the fields and towns of Britain, and from the United States and

Fresh oats for the horses on the
Western Front, 1916
National Library of Scotland

Canada, and shipped to a terrible, frightening world as unfamiliar to them as it was for humans.

At the outbreak of war in August 1914, the British Army was desperate for horses. From the 25,000 they had at the outbreak, a further 150,000 were acquired immediately by compulsory purchase, and within two years the numbers exceeded one million. Government agents visited farms and businesses and commandeered horses area by area. All types were taken, donkeys, riding horses, vanners, and of course, the Clydesdale, needed for the rapidly expanding British Expeditionary Force.

But World War I differed from previous wars. The advent of barbed wire, machine guns and heavy artillery seriously limited the effectiveness of cavalry operations. The Western Front

GUN -TEAMS

Their rugs are sodden, their heads are down,
their tails are turned to the storm :
(Would you know them, you that groomed them in the sleek fat days of peace,
When the tiles rang to their pawings in the lighted stalls, and warm,
Now the foul clay cakes on britching strap and clogs the quick-release ?)

The blown rain stings, there is never a star, the tracks are rivers of slime :
(You must harness-up by guesswork with a failing torch for light,
Instep-deep in unmade standings ; for it's active-service time,
And our resting weeks are over, and we move the guns to-night.)

The iron tyres slither, the traces sag, their blind hooves stumble and slide;
They are war-worn, they are weary, soaked with sweat and sopped with rain:
(You must hold them, you must help them, swing your lead and centre wide
Where the greasy granite pave peters out to squelching drain.)

You have shod them cold, and their coats are long, and their bellies stiff
                                                                with the mud;
They have done with gloss and polish, but the fighting heart's unbroke . . .
We, who saw them hobbling after us down white roads flecked with blood,
Patient, wondering why we left them, till we lost them in the smoke;

Who have felt them shiver between our knees, when the shells rain black
                                                                from the skies,
When the bursting terrors find us and the lines stampede as one;
Who have watched the pierced limbs quiver and the pain in stricken eyes;
Know the worth of humble servants, foolish-faithful to their gun.

Gilbert Frankau, 1884 – 1952
From *The City of Fear and other Poems* Chatto & Windus, London 1918

Frozen watering point on the
Western Front
National Library of Scotland

became the scene of static trench warfare, with some 440 miles of barbed wire and trenches stretching from the Swiss border to the North Sea. As the ground became more and more impassable for motorised vehicles, more and more horses had to be drafted in to move everything, including the soldiers to the front, and the wounded back from it.

Clydesdales were particularly favoured for the heavy artillery guns. It took a team of ten horses to pull a 15 ton Howitzer, and these teams of horses were particularly vulnerable to enemy fire when harnessed to such heavy machinery and unable to seek shelter or relocate quickly.

The rate of loss of horses was as dreadful as for the men. They died of disease and exhaustion. They were drowned in mud, gassed and blown to pieces. Many were wounded or injured and the Army Veterinary Corps was charged with returning any useful horses to the fighting line. Over £250,000 was raised by

Pulling a horse out of a ditch where it was blown by the concussion of a big shell-burst, Near Reutel, Belgium
National Library of Scotland

the RSPCA Fund for Sick and Wounded Horses, through flag days, collection boxes and the sale of the small anthology 'In Aid of Funds for Wounded Horses'. These funds were spent helping to supply and equip thirteen veterinary hospitals with horse ambulances, bandages, medicines, rugs, halters, corn crushers and chaff cutters. Estimates vary as to the numbers treated, but it was certainly over half a million.

Supplying feed for the horses was in itself a problem. A letter from the Director of Supplies in the War Office, early in November 1914, complained that 'draught horses of the Shire of Clydesdale type are not receiving the full authorised ration.'

Dorothy Brooke with some of the 'poor old war heroes' for which her Memorial Hospital was founded
Courtesy of The Brooke

Fodder was in desperately short supply, and what little hay was available was often trampled into the mud or blown away. Horses were standing, knee deep in mud, tied to a picket line with no respite from the driving rain. And the picket lines could be placed, inadvertently, over enemy time bombs.

The Veterinary Corps made great efforts to educate the personnel responsible for the care of the horses. A chief horse-master was appointed to every corps, and subordinate horse-masters to the smaller units. This expertise helped considerably with the management and veterinary care and provided valuable advice to those who were less experienced.

The men at the front had real affection for their horses. Some described how, in the horror of it all, the only 'person' they could talk to was their horse. Many war memoirs describe the awful sight of dead or dying horses. Signaller Jim Crow, 110th Brigade, The Royal Horse Artillery, put into words what many felt. 'We knew what we were there for; them poor devils didn't, did they?' Men somehow accepted that the war was created by humans, but the agonising deaths of innocent animals who were only doing our bidding was morally wrong.

At the end of the war, only 62,000 horses came home to Britain. The British Government decided to sell off thousands of horses and many ended up emaciated and maltreated on the streets of Cairo. It was these old horses, 'dragging out wretched days of toil in the ownership of masters too poor to feed them', mostly well over twenty years of age, that prompted Dorothy Brooke to found the Old War Horse Memorial Hospital in that city in 1934.

Others, in Belgium and France, ended up as meat on the butcher's slab. It was a terrible betrayal after their brave and willing service.

Clydesdale Horse Society promotion in early World War II from *The Scottish Farmer* 1942

THE CLYDESDALE HORSE SOCIETY OF GREAT BRITAIN AND IRELAND

Breeders: In the present National Emergency there is an excellent market for draught horses and a pronounced indication that the demand will continue once the Emergency has passed. Prepare to meet that demand.	The Advantage will be yours.
Farmers: Morning, noon and night the horse is the farmers' best friend. He is always ready; is not dependent on imports for his maintenance; uses up instead of creating a surplus of agricultural produce.	Horses Breed their own Replacements.
Contractors: Costs of Mechanical Haulage are increasing daily and will continue to increase. Statistics prove that for many classes of haulage, horses are by far the cheapest.	Look to your own Interests.
Importers: The Clydesdale is the only British breed of Draught Horses that enjoys an Export Demand. The breed is to be found in every British Colony and many foreign countries.	Ask Yourself Why?

For *STRENGTH, WEIGHT, UTILITY, DIGNITY* and *LASTING ENDURANCE*—
THE CLYDESDALE IS SUPREME!

Full Particulars and Illustrated Brochure can be had on application to the Secretary:—
BERT JARVIS, Clydesdale Horse Society, 93 HOPE ST., GLASGOW, C.2. *Phone: Central* 2230

Land girls in the Lothians, 1943
Scotsman Publications Ltd

Women's Timber Corps taking a
break from timber hauling
National Museums Scotland;
Scottish Life Archive

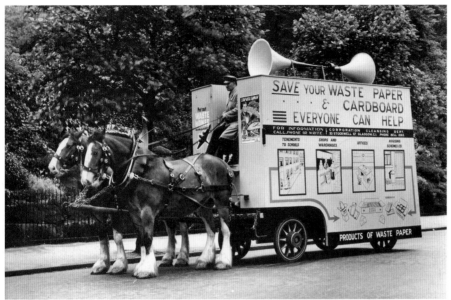

Glasgow Corporation
Cleansing Department
Recycling Appeal
*Culture and Sport
Glasgow (Museums)*

World War II saw our Clydesdale horses in a different kind of service, one which, mercifully, kept them working on their own soil. Draught horses came into their own, as the war found Britain with a serious shortage of work horses. Clydesdale breeding had suffered badly in the 1930s following the withdrawal in 1931 of the Heavy Horse Breeding Grants in Scotland, and the restriction on motor transport, combined with limited availability of petrol, found farmers and contractors paying the highest prices for horses they had seen in twenty years.

Land girls outside Auchincruive
Agricultural College, Ayrshire,
1942
*National Museums Scotland;
Scottish Life Archive*

The huge campaign for increased food production led to massive increases in ploughing and harvesting. 40 per cent more land was under cultivation, and horses were vitally important. The Horse Breeding Grants were reinstated in 1942, which encouraged breeders, and stallion owners, to make the investment in horse power. So many of the smaller farms were once again seen to have mares and foals and the Clydesdale was back at work on the land.

A 'Retrospect and Prospect' written in November 1942 by the then Secretary of State for Scotland, Thomas Johnston, illustrates the urgent nature of the drive for food production:

'As against last year we have 27,000 acres more under potatoes, 88,000 acres more under oats, 14,000 acres more under wheat, and 35,000 acres more under barley. Add other crops, and we have in Scotland an increase over 1941 of 181,000 acres under tillage.

'And despite all the difficulties, the last of the harvest is just coming home. There were fewer casual labourers at the lifting of the potatoes. Nevertheless, one way and another, we had 7,000 more assistants organised. And here I should like to acknowledge the great assistance given us in vital days by the Army authorities. In one area a Corps Commander and a Brigadier turned out in the harvest fields with their total staffs, setting an example to their men. The Women's Land Army, the Education Authorities, everybody helped; our barns and potato pits today are filled, and it is no mere hyperbole to say that the U-boats cannot starve us now.'

The Women's Land Army was re-formed by the government to fill the gap left by male agricultural workers who had joined the forces – over thirty thousand in the first six months of the war. By 1943 there were 80,000 recruits, working on farms and in woods. The Land Girls and Lumber Jills were known as the Forgotten Army, as they took on the role of the traditional farm worker to put food on the nation's tables during the war years.

About one third of these volunteers were from the towns and cities and were relocated to some of the most rural areas, miles from anywhere. Supplied with a basic uniform and a wage of twelve shillings and six pence a week (65p), they rose at dawn to milk cows, spread muck, dig potatoes, and carry bags of grain and bales of hay. And they had to learn to handle the horses, and many became so fond of their charges that they were broken hearted at the end of the war when they had to leave them. One described her struggles to put the heavy collar on – 'I was very short and the horse was extremely large, and he kept tossing his head up and down!' But they had to get on with it, often to the teasing and amusement of the other farm workers. One was told 'you've got that mare wasted' because she covered the horse's head in the rain. 'She didn't like getting her ears wet!' was the girl's reasoning. Her kindness paid off; like many other city girls she stayed on the land and became a farmer's wife!

One recruit, at 4feet 11inches, was told she was 'too wee' to join the Timber Corps. But she proved them all wrong, and working her horse, was one of many who helped keep British industry going through large scale tree felling and extraction.

Due to petrol rationing and manufacturing restrictions, the horse remained important for town and city transportation all through the war years. Glasgow Corporation put their Cleansing Department Clydesdales to good use in their recycling campaign, entreating the population to 'Save your waste food and help to Save your Bacon', or 'Save your Waste Paper and Cardboard, everyone can help' by means of loudspeakers on horse-drawn carts. One ton of kitchen waste per week provided food for forty pigs, a message that reinforced the traditional Scottish values of thrift and supporting the war effort at every level.

The revival in Clydesdale breeding during the war years proved to be short lived. Although the numbers registered in the Clydesdale Stud Book of 1945 were 998 mares and 1437 foals, compared with 768 mares and 1254 foals in 1940, by 1946 the numbers had again decreased. As farmers and contractors took advantage of mechanisation after the war, large numbers of Clydesdales became surplus to requirements and many were bought by horse slaughterers, including young horses with years of breeding and work prospects ahead of them. Well into the 1950s Clydesdale enthusiasts implored farmers and breeders to keep horses, expressing concern at the prospect of a shortage of work horses 'should the nation ever again be faced with a serious emergency comparable to that of 1939.' But the difficulty of finding labour willing to look after horses on evenings and weekends, together with the convenience and novelty of the tractor and lorry, only furthered the decline of the Clydesdale. In the eyes of many, the horse had outlived his usefulness.

Seeding on Dyment Farms, Nanton, Alberta, 1915
Glenbow Archives NA-2685-23

6. Workhorse of the world:
the Clydesdale internationally

'I have seen the Clydesdale under many conditions and
in many lands. I have seen him starting the five-ton
trucks on the wharf at Cape Town, where the mule
teams passing seemed to make him a giant by contrast; I
have seen him girth-deep in the swamps of the
Australian river-roads pulling in the wagon chains as
though his heart would burst; I have seen him amid the
cheers of a dense crowd stepping gaily in the
amphitheatre at the Chicago shows, but here only in
this beautiful silent valley did he seem to be thoroughly
and emphatically at home.'

Judging Clydesdale horses,
Dominion Exhibition, Calgary,
Alberta, 1908
Glenbow Archives NA-2913-6

WILL H Ogilvie wrote the tribute on the previous page in 1908, recording his love for the draught-horse of the Borders, and the wholly Scottish identity of 'the white-blazed faces and the active, feathered feet'.

Scotland is rightly proud of her many exports and inventions. Bicycles, pneumatic tyres, waterproof mackintoshes and whisky are just some of them. From our small country also came the Clydesdale, which over the years became the finest draught horse breed in the history of the world. Not content with winning favour with buyers in England, Wales and Ireland, from the 1880s the Clydesdale was exported to Australia, Canada, the United States, Russia, South America and South Africa. The total number exported had reached over 19,500 by 1930.

The first Clydesdale stallion was imported to Canada in 1840. Cumberland, ironically an English name, went to Western Ontario, and others followed. Such was the enthusiasm for the Clydesdale that numbers imported and bred led to the first Canadian Stud Book in 1886 which contained 563 horses, of which 243 were mares. The Clydesdale Horse Association of Canada made every effort to improve and establish the breed by importing high quality animals and breeding selectively. At the same time as many Scots were headed for new lives in

Canada, their own native draught horse was also making his way over the Atlantic, sailing from the Clyde to Halifax and Montreal. By the beginning of the twentieth century the Western Provinces had over 200,000 working horses, of which the Clydesdale was indisputably the most popular. While in Eastern Canada the Clydesdale was in demand for logging, it was on the Prairies of Alberta, Manitoba, and Saskatchewan that he gained the lasting acknowledgement that the breed 'opened up Western Canada'. Over 50,000 pedigreed Clydesdales were registered in Canada before World War II, a great many imported before the 1914 war had made the journey hazardous. One famous imported stallion, McQueen, belonging to Graham Brothers, died aged 26 having served over 1,700 mares and left over 1,000 foals in his lifetime. Even the Prince of Wales, later to become the Duke of Windsor, owned a ranch near Calgary where he bred Clydesdales from the very best bloodlines.

Doondodge Mossrock, 19 hands high, bred by John McCubbing at Drum Farm, Beeswing, Dumfries. Held by son Alexander at Unity, Saskatchewan in 1933. The girl on his back is Dorothy Myfanwy Little
Courtesy of Lorna McCubbin

While Percherons and Belgians were also popular, it was the Clydesdale that dominated. The work required to cultivate the vast acreage of arable land led to use of large teams of horses, often up to twelve at a time, to maximise the economic benefit and cover more acreage with fewer men. A team like this could plant up to eighty acres a day, or, depending on the soil conditions, plough eight acres a day using a three furrow plough.

Jerry Wismer spreading manure with a pair of mares, 1984. Clydeslea Dianna on the right was one of the first Clydesdales he owned, and her daughter Cedarlane Heather is on the left
Courtesy of Gerald Wismer

Solomon's Commodore with a Wismer son working on each leg before winning the Grand Champion Stallion at the 1981 Michigan Great Lakes Show. His owner, Richard Wegner, in the cowboy hat, is on the left. This stallion was the sire of Cedarlane Heather
Courtesy of Gerald Wismer

Mechanisation and the tractor had begun to take their toll on horse numbers by the 1930s, but the Depression had a dire effect on Canada's farmlands. A major drought combined with the economic downturn led to widespread poverty. As tractor imports fell from over 20,000 in 1929 to under 2,000 in 1933, and petrol was unaffordable, the only answer was to return the horse to his former position as the essential worker on the prairies. The result was that horse numbers fell less dramatically in Western Canada during these years than might otherwise have been expected. But the combination of World War II and the development of new tractors saw massive displacement of horses. Slaughter plants were established and by 1949 more than 18,000 tons of horse meat was being canned and shipped to Europe.

Not all the Clydesdales met this grisly fate; many found their way back to the Eastern Provinces for work in the timber industry. And men like Tom Devlin, a Secretary of the Clydesdale Horse Association of Canada, worked tirelessly to ensure that the Clydesdale would continue to thrive and grow in the Dominion.

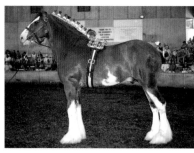

S B H Phoenix, foaled 18th March 1998. This stallion, owned by Wismer Clydes, has won 25 Champion and Reserve Championships in his showing career, and is a 3-time All-American and All-Canadian winner. He has sired 19 All-American winners since 2003
Courtesy of Gerald Wismer

Big names in Clydesdales over the years have been Wreford Hewson, who worked and showed Clydesdales his entire life, David Carson of Carson Farms, who not only breeds and shows but holds regular horse auctions, and the Ridlers of Maple Stone Farm. Further west the Cey family have been breeding black Clydesdales for three generations, and in 2010 imported Doura Dewridge Douglas from Jim Young in Scotland. Jerry Wismer is President of the Clydesdale Horse Association of Canada, and has bred Clydesdales for well over thirty years. A better ambassador for the breed would be hard to find, with his stallion S B H Phoenix, purchased from the Priebes in Michigan in 1999, siring numerous prize winners in North America. Not only is his semen widely exported, four of his sons and one grandson

Danielle Lewis driving a pair of Clydesdales with a Disc Harrow. Lewisview Farm Fun Day, Markham, Ontario, 2010
Photo Lynn Caldwell

have been sold to Scotland including Great American G W Carver to John Anderson's Redcastle Stud and Spartan Lad, now known as Jackton's Discovery, to Jim Steel at Jackton, East Kilbride. Phoenix's son Cedarlane Thunder was the first Clydesdale to be exported from North America to Germany in January 2010.

Marion Young is the daughter of John Young of Doura Clydesdales fame. In 1976 she started travelling to Canada to deliver horses, and by 1982 it seemed only sensible to set up in business there, in Listowel, Ontario. She moved to Hanover in 2003, and in the same year started the journal *The Clydesdale Speculator*. Still actively facilitating imports from Scotland, she is also an international judge and enthusiastic encourager on 'all things Clydesdale'.

Covered Bridge Beauty, a joint entry of John Newell (Ontario) and Schuler Farms (Alabama, USA), winner of the Clydesdale Mare Cart Class at the 2010 Royal Agricultural Winter Fair, Toronto. Driven by Gordon Carruthers
Photo Lynn Caldwell

SOUTH of the border, the Clydesdale Breeders Association of the United States was formed in 1879, coinciding with the increase in imports to meet the demands of expanding agriculture. Their first stud book was published in 1882, listing over 1,000 mares and stallions. Leading lights of the early Clydesdale importing days were Colonel Holloway of Illinois and Alex Galbraith, an immigrant from Stirlingshire to Wisconsin.

It was not only on the farms of the great plains that Clydesdales proved their worth. Horse teams were needed to deliver heavy goods in the cities, and hitches of two, four or six were used depending on the weight of the load. Six horse hitches became popular for public relations purposes in a number of industries, and competition was fierce between companies regarding the quality and turnout of their horse teams. Few sights

Budweiser Clydesdales at home in St. Louis

were more popular with the public than a hitch of six Clydesdales, with gleaming coats and high stepping feathered legs, pulling heavy loads on wagons which themselves weighed up to two tons.

Nathan Goff of Clarksburg, West Virginia, was one of many enthusiastic importers of quality Clydesdales. A frequent visitor to the Lanark sales, he was usually a buyer. Not only did he maintain a large stud of breeding Clydesdales, he was a regular exhibitor with his six-horse team at both Canadian and United States shows.

One of the greatest ambassadors for the Clydesdale breed has undoubtedly been Anheuser-Busch, Inc., of St. Louis, Missouri, who has successfully promoted both Budweiser beers and the now famous Budweiser Clydesdales. Such was the

Budweiser Clydesdale with friend

enthusiasm of the Busch family that they purchased and shipped many horses every year; in 1955 alone the consignment was five stallions, two fillies and three geldings. And they bore losses with fortitude. In the early 1940s eight Clydesdales, specially selected for Anheuser-Busch by James Kilpatrick, set sail for North America on the *Salaria*. The ship was torpedoed and sunk by German U-boats. Undaunted, another shipment was arranged in 1953 which included ten females, one stallion and four geldings, laying the foundations of the Anheuser-Busch breeding programme. While they still buy from Scotland, the company's policy of home breeding led to the establishment in 2008 of a new state-of-the-art breeding farm in Cooper County, Missouri. Today Anheuser-Busch own around 250 Clydesdales, and their hitches make hundreds of public appearances every year. Their Super Bowl promotional advertising spots have become a cult hit on the internet.

The pivotal role played by the United States in the world of Clydesdales is demonstrated by their hosting of the World Clydesdale Show. The 2007 show was held in Madison, Wisconsin and had over 600 horses on show with nearly 15,000 visitors. The 2011 event will be held in the same venue.

A National Clydesdale Sale is held every year, drawing horses and buyers from all over North America. A measure of the demand for these horses was demonstrated in 2008 when the top seller made $20,000, and seven were sold to Brazil.

THE FIRST Clydesdales were exported to Australia in the 1850s, although Governor Phillip had requested that draught horses be sent as early as 1792. The first shipments were a mix of breeds, including Cleveland Bays and Suffolk Punches, but the discovery of gold in New South Wales and Victoria in the 1850s established the need for the best heavy horses. With the gold rush, particularly in Victoria, there came a rapid growth in immigration and settlements. Heavy horses were needed to cart materials.

The long journey from Britain, often taking several months, was hard on the horses and, of course, some failed to complete it. But the result was that only the best and hardiest of stock was imported and the Clydesdale adapted well to his new land.

The work was demanding and the distances great. Land had to be cleared, timber hauled, and dams dug to provide water supplies. Heavy loads of grain and wool were hauled by teams, sometimes of up to twenty six horses. And the pressure on farming, to feed a growing population, led to the use of ever larger and heavier farm equipment to maximise production. The Clydesdale had come into his own.

Although a Draught Horse Stud Book of Australia was in existence from 1907, the Australian Clydesdale Horse Society did not publish its first volume until 1917. In 1918 the Clydesdale section of the Draught Horse Stud Book was included and a new organisation, the Commonwealth Clydesdale Horse Society of Australia, was established. Love for and pride in the breed grew and local shows became popular as a means of displaying the best horses.

The peak of Clydesdale numbers in Australia was not reached until the 1930s. The depression had only added to the delay in mechanisation and good horses were still in great demand. Cargo ships with up to twenty horses on board sailed from Liverpool to be met on the docks by enthusiastic bidders. Men like David Adam and Hugh McGregor made it their business to bring the horses off ship in prime condition; no mean feat when the length of the journey and the cramped conditions on board are taken into account.

Two Clydesdales pulling a traditional Australian Drovers wagon
Courtesy of Katy Driver

The start of World War II in 1939 was the beginning of a very dark period for heavy horses. Although the horse was still in demand as a source of power, especially after petrol rationing was introduced in 1940, the horse market fell away after 1945. Some farmers argued that the horse was indispensable, but gradually mechanisation took over and there were large numbers of horses for sale and no one to buy them. Young horses were

David Martin ploughing with
Coolibah Ridge Jasper and
Lavereen Clem, Queensland,
Australia
Courtesy of Katy Driver

going for less than two pounds a head, and some were simply turned loose to fend for themselves.

For some families, the Clydesdale teams were kept on and breeding and showing became the tradition that was to enable the Clydesdale to recover enough to stage a comeback. Families like the Cox's Valmont Stud, and the Marriotts, both in Victoria, have become internationally famous through their acquisition and breeding of the finest bloodlines. From Scottish imports such as Craigie Superb, and more recently Greendykes Benjie, to their own home-bred stock, Australia can lay claim to some of the finest Clydesdales in the world. Shane and Andrea Fuchsbichler, of Redbrook Clydesdales in Gidgegannup in Western Australia, have recently imported from Robert Hamilton and from Charles Carrick, adding to an already impressive stud.

Major brewers such as Coopers continue to use Clydesdales, keeping the breed in the public eye. New converts to the breed are purchasing horses for breeding, showing, and working. Riding Clydesdales and Clydesdale crosses has become increasingly popular. There is even a Clydesdale Cross Sports Horse Association.

Almost 30,000 Clydesdales have been bred in Australia since 1924 when the stud book was first published. The horse is held in such esteem that he has been called 'the horse that laid the foundation of Australia', or as the Commonwealth Clydesdale Horse Society puts it 'The Breed That Built a Nation'. Statues in tribute to the Clydesdale are to be seen in several states, including Merredin, Western Australia, Angaston, South Australia, and a sculpture in Boonah, Queensland by Glasgow

The XXXX Brewery Clydesdale Team in front of the Breakfast Creek Hotel in Brisbane
Courtesy of Katy Driver

What the Fuchsbichler family from Gidgegannup, Western Australia, do when it's too hot to do anything else!
Courtesy of Redbrook Clydesdales

Dillars Spectacular, Supreme Champion 2010 at Perth Royal Show for Redbrook Clydesdales, Western Australia
Courtesy of Redbrook Clydesdales

artist Andy Scott. Entitled 'Clydebuilt', the inscription reads: 'This statue stands as a tribute to the Clydesdale heavy horse and the role it played in the development of our Nation.'

'Clydebuilt' steel sculpture in Boonah, Queensland by Glasgow artist Andy Scott.
'This statue stands as a tribute to the Clydesdale heavy horse and the role it
played in the development of our Nation.'
Photo Dan Proud, Courtesy of Scenic Rim Regional Council, Queensland

Cottle Farms Alice with a newborn colt, 'Highgrounds', Timaru, New Zealand
Courtesy of the Cottle family

NEW ZEALAND found Clydesdales to be the best horses for all types of agricultural work. From the pioneering days to mechanisation, the Clydesdale dominated the landscape. Whether it was setting up grain-growing farms on the East Coast of the North and South Islands, road building and carting, or hauling loads on wagons, the horse was the main source of power. The earliest imports recorded were in 1860, and in 1911 came the call to form a Clydesdale Horse Society of New Zealand. The first Stud Book was published in 1914 with over 2,000 entries.

From the 1920s New Zealand experienced a similar decline in horse numbers to other parts of the world as motorised transport and tractors took over. The reduction in numbers was so serious that in the 1950s the Clydesdale in New Zealand was declared a rare breed. But some farmers never gave up on their

Leaders of a 6 horse plough team
Courtesy of the Cottle family

Mares and young horses in snow at the
Cottle farm, waiting to be fed
Courtesy of the Cottle family

Emma and Sarah Kent with two
Clydesdale sisters at Ashburton
Show, Canterbury, New Zealand,
2009
Courtesy of Sue Butterick-Kent

The DB Draught Clydesdales
(owned by Pirongia Clydesdales) in
Christchurch, New Zealand
Courtesy of Pirongia Clydesdales

Clydesdales and the Society and Stud Book have been
continued. Sue Butterick-Kent's family arrived in New
Zealand in the 1860s from Yorkshire and since then
they have continuously kept, worked and bred Clydesdales. And the Cottle family have never gone out of
Clydesdales. They are still used for the majority of farm
work, up to nine at a time for ploughing with a four
furrow plough.

Pirongia Clydesdales began life as the DB Breweries
Draught Clydesdale Team in 1985. Nick and Jill van
der Sande maintained the team of six matching black
Clydesdales for the brewery, and they travelled all over
New Zealand with a beautifully presented brewery
wagon and a Dalmatian dog. However, despite the popularity of the Clydesdales with the public, in 1999 DB
decided to stop using the horses to promote their beer.

Nick and Jill decided that, after all their years of
experience managing the team, they would continue
with the team in a new privately owned venture based
in the village of Pirongia. Now, ten years later, Pirongia
Clydesdales is now a centre of attraction with a working
horse museum, a café, an all-weather arena, and a
training facility for harness driving. And the horses are
as popular as ever for weddings, street parades, and
VIP events.

As in Australia, there is a growing interest in
Clydesdales and Clyde crosses for riding and some agri-
cultural shows now have classes specifically for ridden
Clydesdales.

(opposite) Duncan and Hamish Cottle
with a team of four in the DB Mainland
Brewery wagon in Timaru, South
Island, New Zealand
Courtesy of the Cottle family

Talisman Farms Megan, owned by
Talisman Farms Sport Horses, near
Masterton, New Zealand
Courtesy of Louise Wilsden

The first Clydesdales were exported to Argentina in the 1870s, and over the years both Montgomery and Kilpatrick studs sent consignments. Montgomery also supplied many of the 150 sent to the Cape Town Harbour Board, South Africa, in 1901. In 1886 Clydesdales were exported to Russia, where they were crossed with native mares to create a new breed of very heavy draught horse. A further 16, also from Montgomery, were shipped in 1904.

Dame Marie McGregor with his mother Varrie, the first Clydesdale foal born on the Dame Marie Stud, St Philbert de Bouaine in Western France

Clydesdales, not surprisingly, also found their way to Ireland where they have been popular since the middle of the nineteenth century. The Clydesdale influence is readily seen in the popular Irish Draught horse, and pure bred Clydesdales have been successfully bred and shown all over Ireland. It is a matter of some pride that the prestigious Cawdor Cup for the best female at the Royal Highland Show in 2010 went home to Coleraine, for Alex and Geoffrey Tanner's three year old Woodhouse Sunshine.

EUROPE has consistently been a market, albeit a small one. Given the existence of powerful European breeds, the Belgian and the Percheron, the Clydesdale has enough charm and character to win the hearts and minds of buyers in Germany, Sweden, Holland and Denmark, with nearly twenty horses leaving the UK for these countries in the last two years. And a small organisation calling itself 'France Clydesdale' has been established to promote the breed in that country where at present there is only one Clydesdale Stud.

The Clydesdale continues to win hearts in new territories. Phil Farrell, a farmer from Illinois, sent his first consignment of six horses to China in March 2010. A big Chinese dairy owner is planning to use Clydesdales in promoting his brand.

Cathcart Lofty saddled for action
Courtesy of Samantha Weir

7. Ride a real horse: the ridden Clydesdale

CLYDESDALES have always been ridden. Horsemen returning from outlying fields usually rode back to the farm at 'lousin' time' for pragmatic reasons; why walk a mile when you can get a lift? Many rode side-saddle style just for the ease of it, but the draught horse took kindly to his handler sitting on his back as he plodded home at the end of the day's work.

The Irvine Carters Society was formed in 1753, a recognition by the town council of their role in the growth and prosperity of Irvine as a sea port. Their annual parade through the Ayrshire town became part of the festival of Mary's Mass, which has been celebrated as Marymass continuously in August each year. Clydesdales dominate the parade through the town, and the oldest continuous Clydesdale race takes place on the moor in

Farm horsemen homeward bound,
Scottish Borders
*The Robert D. Clapperton
Photographic Trust*

Clydesdale racing at Marymass,
Irvine
Courtesy of Julie Affleck

Samantha Weir rounding up cattle on her 4 year old Clydesdale stallion Cathcart Lofty, Goulburn, New South Wales, Australia
Courtesy of Samantha Weir

the afternoon. These races have their origins in the carters' trade. Only horses that had taken part in the parade were raced, and the results established the fittest horses for the subsequent buying and selling. Now, in the twenty first century, the sight and sound of galloping Clydesdales is a continuing feature of the Marymass Festival and a reminder of the tradition of the ridden carthorse.

However the concept of the Clydesdale as a ridden horse in the general equestrian sphere is relatively recent. One of the earliest enthusiasts was Annie Rose, who started her heavy horse business on the Isle of Skye nearly ten years ago. Originally working a dray, Annie was convinced that the Clydesdale had real potential as a fantastic riding horse, and she set about making her dream come true by promoting West Highland Heavy Horses as a Riding Centre. Not 'pony trekking', but varied and instructional rides which encouraged experienced riders and ensured that the horses were well schooled and responsive.

The Skye location proved to be both a blessing, in the shape of wonderful scenery, and a disadvantage due to the sheer distance from most potential customers. A combination of marketing genius and practical planning led to 'The Great Clydesdale Migration' in 2006, which saw ten horses undertake

Clydesdale racing at Marymass, Irvine
Courtesy of Julie Affleck

the epic ride from Skye to the Whicham Valley in Cumbria, a journey of 420 miles. Customers paid to take part in different sections of the ride, sponsors were found and the entire journey was filmed for television and a subsequent DVD. The logistics of route planning and accommodation finding, and the trials of weather and terrain, all proved enormously worthwhile in the resulting publicity which established Cumbrian Heavy Horses as a major British Horse Society Approved equestrian centre and tourist attraction. Annie and her team have built on this so successfully that, in 2010, Cumbrian Heavy Horses won the Best Tourist Experience Award, not only at home in Cumbria but they then went on to win the Award for England's North West.

A Cumbrian Fell ride
Courtesy of Cumbrian Heavy Horses

Beach gallop
Courtesy of Cumbrian Heavy Horses

Courtesy of Cumbrian Heavy Horses

Baremuir Superior (Buddy) plays football at a 'Horseboy Camp' for autistic children
Photo Gillian Naysmith

The popularity of Clydesdales as ridden horses has been matched by the growth in show classes for Clydesdales under saddle at agricultural and horse shows. The Royal Highland Show held a class for ridden Clydesdales for the first time in 2006, and a Ridden Clydesdale Championship is held in August each year at the Blair Castle International Horse Trials in Perthshire.

Pamela Duncan's Clydesdale stallion Baremuir Superior, known to his fan club as Buddy, has broken the mould when it comes to ridden Clydesdales. He stood at stud until he was ten years old, when Pamela bought him and broke him to ride. Always convinced that Clydesdales would make excellent riding horses, Pamela has proved in this unique partnership just what is possible with the combination of temperament, athleticism and versatility of the breed. Not content with winning the Novice One Day Event at Burgie in Moray in August 2010, Buddy has recently become a 'Horseboy' horse at camps for autistic children.

Blair Castle Ridden Clydesdale
Championship
Courtesy of Pamela Duncan

Clydesdale stallion Baremuir
Superior on his way to winning the
Burgie Novice One Day Event,
2010
Photo Graham Clement

The enthusiasm for riding Clydesdales is international. Ridden Clydesdales make their appearance at the Calgary Stampede and the World Clydesdale Show and competitions of all sizes in numerous locations all over the world testify to the growing popularity and versatility of Scotland's native draught horse.

Samantha Weir from the Misty Park Stud at Goulburn, NSW, Australia, also pays tribute to 'the temperament of these fantastic horses'. Samantha rode Clydesdales from her childhood when she first outgrew her Shetland pony and competed in all pony club events and agricultural shows including jumping, cross country and dressage. She says:

'My close relationship with my Clydesdales has led me to compete and ride in the UK and around the globe. One of my favourite competitions was when I was awarded best turned-out heavy hunter at the Royal Highland Show in 2003, riding sidesaddle on Sir Lancelot of Strathorn 'Jake', a purebred Clydesdale gelding owned by Ruth and George Skinner from Strathorn Farm, Aberdeenshire. This was the first time a purebred heavy horse had ever competed at the Royal Highland Show under saddle. 'Jake' was also placed third in the single horse four-wheeled turnout that afternoon.

'Another personal highlight was the opportunity of riding Doug and Kathy Lindsey's super Clydesdale mare 'Dee' at the World Clydesdale Show in 2007 in Madison, Wisconsin. This was also a sidesaddle riding demonstration showing the versatility, athleticism and grace of the purebred Clydesdale. Dee had never carried a sidesaddle prior to the show (I flew my sidesaddle with me from Australia), she had a quick fitting and ride the night before. The next day she walked, trotted and cantered around the arena like she had done it all her life. That evening she also won the Clydesdale Ridden (Youth) at the World Clydesdale Show and has gone on to win the American Champion Ridden.'

Sir Lancelot of Strathorn (Jake)
ridden sidesaddle by Samantha
Weir at the 2003 Royal Highland
Show
Courtesy of Samantha Weir

Samantha Weir riding 'Dee' at the
World Clydesdale Show, Madison,
2007
Courtesy of Samantha Weir

Kathy Lindsey riding 'Dee' in the Clydesdale Ridden (English) class at the World Clydesdale Show
Courtesy of Samantha Weir

Louise Wilsden runs Talisman Farm Sport Horses in Masterton, New Zealand, aiming to produce 'extraordinary horses for ordinary riders'. For some years Kintyre Lodge Robbie, a purebred Clydesdale stallion, stood at stud there, and Louise has only good things to say about the breed. As she says, 'The Clydesdale has a work ethic that translates exceptionally well under saddle and it is this combination of sensible temperament and desire to please with a not inconsiderable amount of physical power that can produce a surprisingly athletic and sound animal. The Clydesdale is also a breed whose inherent toughness means that it does well living out 24/7, which is how a great many horses in NZ live.

Samantha Van Der Sande of Pirongia Clydesdales riding Claremont Mark at the Morrinsville A & P Show, New Zealand
Courtesy of Pirongia Clydesdales

'I currently ride a purebred Clydesdale, Talisman Farms Megan. I bred this mare with express desire to produce her under saddle and demonstrate the breed's ability, in its pure form, to be an active and competitive pleasure mount. My girl is only three years old but in her first competition, a dressage series, she was consistently in the top quarter of the field and even won one of her tests.'

Talisman Farms Megan ridden by Louise Wilsden at home
in New Zealand
Courtesy of Louise Wilsden

Wendee Cristante from British Columbia, Canada, was so convinced of the versatility and agility of Clydesdale horses that she established The Canadian Clyde Ride Team in 2000. She and her all female team of riders trained the horses to perform precision moves to music, and launched the world's first draught horse musical ride in Vancouver in 2001. Many sceptics said it

The Canadian Clyde Ride Team
Photos Eric Jensen, Vancouver, B.C.
Courtesy of Dee Wendee Cristante

couldn't be done, but Dee quotes George Bernard Shaw – 'people who say it cannot be done. . . should never interrupt those who are doing it!' Her now famous choreographed dancing Clydesdales have been Champions at the Calgary Stampede, appeared at Disneyland, and represented Canada at the New Years Day Tournament of Roses in Pasadena, California.

Strathorn Farm Musical Drill Ride
Skinner family collection

Mac and Jim, two purebred
Clydesdales from Strathorn Farm,
on duty as police horses in
Holyrood Park, Edinburgh
Skinner family collection

Sally Anne Oultram riding Ted
Oultram family collection

At Strathorn Farm Stables in Aberdeenshire, the musical drill ride has become a favourite feature of their annual Heavy Horse Open Day. The themed drill, featuring Clydesdales, is another demonstration of the horse's versatility and grace by the Skinner family, who were also the first to show one of their Clydesdales under side saddle at the Royal Highland Show.

The same stables were the source of two pure bred Clydesdale horses sold to Lothian and Borders Police in 2004. Not surprisingly, Clydesdales and Clydesdale crosses are well suited to police work, where the primary requirements are for medium to heavy weight horses at least 16 hands in height. The calm and equable temperament, combined with courage and willingness to please, has won them plaudits from police forces from Scotland to Southampton. In a typical year Strathclyde Mounted Branch horses help police over 100 football matches, while a Clydesdale cross called Trooper served for 16 years with the Lothian and Borders service, including the demonstrations in Edinburgh during the 2005 G8 Summit.

And, as befits our world's workhorse, he is also to be found in the Mounted Unit for New Castle County Police, Wilmington, Delaware, USA, where 6 of their 8 horses are Clydesdales. One of these, Commander, pulled an ice cream cart before becoming a police horse, and another, Darby, has been placed first on two occasions in the National Police Equestrian Championships.

Danielle Lewis jumping her
Clydesdale gelding 'Handsome',
Markham, Ontario, Canada
Photo Lynn Caldwell

Sally Anne Oultram is a Trustee of the Rare Breeds Survival Trust and she and her Clydesdale Ted are Ambassadors for RBST. She is a firm believer in the Clydesdale as a riding horse and emphasizes the importance of their new role in the future health of the breed. Previously classified as 'At Risk', the Clydesdale is still regarded as a 'Vulnerable' breed, and Sally Anne is convinced that the growth of interest in the Clydesdale as a riding horse is ensuring that 'these beautiful horses will not be lost forever.'

Those who have had the pleasure of riding one of these magnificent animals will agree with Sir Winston Churchill, who said: 'When you are on a great horse, you have the best seat you will ever have.'

David Wise ploughing at
Sillywrea, Northumberland March
2010
Dodd and Wise family collection

John Dodd coming home from
work, Sillywrea, Northumberland
Dodd and Wise family collection

8. Working today

Och a coo's jist a coo, and a sheep's jist a sheep.
Tho' it's maybe a lamb tae begin wi'!
An' a pig in a sty ye can scent walkin' by,
And he's no jist a pet ye can rin' wi!

A dog's guid tae ken if he's pleasant and wise,
An' a decent companion in action.
But if ye are thirled tae the animal world
It's the horse that's your greatest attraction.

In fact it's the horse that takes a'body's e'e,
No only the fermer himsel', man.
He's ever a draw in street, showyard an' a',
An' harnessed, he aye rings the bell, man.

Adam Hardie

POPULAR opinion has implied, in the last few decades, that the day of the Clydesdale is done and that they are no more than sentimental ornaments, or a plaything for those rich enough to continue to breed and show them as a hobby. And there is no doubt that such people kept the horse going in the lean years from the 1950s onwards when the lorry and the tractor had largely supplanted native horse power. But quietly, and without fanfare, some dedicated horsemen have continued to work with horses, and firmly believe that their use is justified on both economic and environmental grounds.

John Dodd and his son in law David Wise are just such men. On Sillywrea, the family farm in Northumberland, they work their 200 acres with Clydesdale horses in the same way they have done for generations. Exceptions are made for specific jobs such as baling hay and straw, where David has bought a

John Dodd turning hay with Sandy
Dodd and Wise family collection

Richard Wise, the next generation, with Jock at Sillywrea in 2004
Dodd and Wise family collection

baler and borrows a tractor to drive it, but all the general work on the farm is done by the horses. To John, horses offer maximum flexibility, as he says, 'You can work six horses as a team, as three pairs or six singles. You can't split a tractor!' They have seven horses, 'too many!' says John, but there are good reasons for it. Ideally they would have four working horses with a young one coming on, but nowadays it's harder to find replacements. In the past they would buy at Clydesdale sales, but now most are sold privately.

Traditionally Sillywrea have bought their Clydesdales as colt foals, which are cheaper when not show quality. They always have a young horse to break, which ensures continuity as the working team gets older or if any of them go lame. Their older horses used to be sold on to lighter work on other small farms, but there aren't so many of those now either.

But even buying as foals, horses are not a cheap option. If you buy a colt foal for a thousand pounds, and add the costs of transport, castration, and feeding, by the time you have a work horse at three or four years old you've made a significant investment. But compared with thirty or forty thousand pounds for a tractor, it's good value when a horse can work for fifteen years or more.

Richard Wise, David's son and John's grandson, is in his final year at Kirkley Hall College near Ponteland, and is as enthusiastic about the horses as his father and grandfather. As part of his course he chose to analyse comparative costs, and believes that he proved that farming with horses can be more economical. As the only student on the course with hands-on family experience of farming with horses, his concern for the future is finding appropriate training for anyone who wants to work the land with horses. In his view, the equestrian courses in horse management simply don't meet the need when it comes to working with heavy horses as they are designed for employment in riding schools and livery yards.

All three men love their horses and are proud of the work they do. Twelve acres of hay can be cut in a day, working 4am to

9pm using two pairs of horses, and one horse, Winston, can turn twelve acres of hay in four hours. As the horses are worked every day, they are kept fit, and John and David ensure that all their horse-drawn implements are kept in good condition by using them in rotation to prevent rust.

Love of the land lies at the heart of this family farm, and John, the patriarch, has been known to turn to poetry to express himself as in this excerpt from 'Son of the Soil'.

Up and down the fertile sod
The strong and steady horses plod
With nodding heads and tight-drawn chains
Guided with light hand on the reins.

The ploughman with his steady gait
Guides the plough so true and straight
And as he walks with measured stride
Doing his work with love and pride
Not a dull and humble ploughman
But a proud and happy yeoman.

As he does each task in season
His life unfolds with rhyme and reason
Only the ignorant think his work is dull
His joy: the singing lark and wheeling gull
The fallow greening with the sprouting corn
The mists in hollows on a summer's morn.

And as he tends his fields, the hoof, the horn
He thinks: Oh who is man that he should mourn?
For man like grass is gone tomorrow
To misuse God's land a greater sorrow.

ON THE OTHER SIDE of the world, in Timaru, New Zealand, the Cottle family continue to farm over 500 acres in the South Island working almost entirely with Clydesdale horses.

Duncan Cottle ploughing with a 9 horse team in a 4 furrow plough and equalising rope and block hitch
Courtesy of the Timaru Herald

John Cottle's enthusiasm for horses began when he was a boy in the 1950s and he and his brother Grahame used a horse and sledge for feeding livestock and for carting cream from the cowshed to the road to be picked up by the cream lorry. His interest in Clydesdales grew and in the 1960s he enrolled Bill McLeavy, a well known draught horse man, as his friend and mentor in helping him select the best horses for his breeding stock. He built up his horse numbers to enable him to have two five-horse teams by the 1970s, and he used them to break in virgin swamp land.

Geoffrey Cottle driving 3 abreast in the farm wagon to feed out-wintered stock in the winter of 2006
Courtesy of the Cottle family

The horses continued to do most of the agricultural work on the dairy, pig and arable farm, although a tractor was bought in the 1970s. All the ploughing, discing, grubbing, harrowing, rolling, sowing and hay making was done by the horses, who were fed on the oaten chaff which was grown and made on the farm every year.

In 1989 John and his family moved farms from Levin in the North Island to Timaru in the South Island, a distance of approximately 500 kilometres, using only the horses for transport. Five horses pulled the wagon which the family lived in, and another horse was hitched to a cart loaded with chaff which carried the farm dogs underneath. The four Cottle children rode their own Welsh ponies. The family camped at riverbeds overnight, feeding the horses with chaff in a tarpaulin strung between the shafts of the wagon. The horses were either tied on a rope line or kept within an electric fence at night.

The journey took eighteen days, varying the distances according to access to water, and some days they did not travel at all. There were sound practical reasons for making the trip in this way. There was a time lapse between giving up possession on the old property and taking over the new one, and it was a good way of keeping the horses fit and in work.

John and his family still breed and use Clydesdales for the majority of their farm work. Teams of up to nine plough with a 4 furrow plough, and eight work abreast for a set of 16 inch discs. The Cottle's horses also do promotional work in parades for the local Mainland Brewery.

Debates continue on the value of working farms with horses, becoming more lively with each passing decade and with every publicised trend in oil prices or climate change. Those who make it work for them, like the Cottle family and John Dodd and his family, are still unusual in the early twenty first century, but there are others who see a place for horses on a working farm even if they are not the sole means of power.

Sherry Lewis driving two black Clydesdale geldings with a buck rake, Lewisview Farm, Markham, Ontario
Photo Lynn Caldwell

FARRIER Stephen Jones from Campbeltown, Argyll, undertook a caravan holiday, pulled by his Clydesdale cross and he has experience of using horses on upland farmland. The advantages, he says, are particularly in carting feed to outwintered cattle and sheep, where the ground is too wet to use a tractor and using the horse allows the feeding to be in a different place every day and prevents the ground being poached. He also enthuses about the benefits of a horse and cart for feeding and bedding in the yard. 'I just load the cart and go down the middle feed passage stopping at the first pen. I climb on to the load and throw the bales into the pen, and just tell the horse to move up. Once he knows his job the horse will automatically stop at the next pen. It's much quicker than a tractor because you don't have to keep climbing on and off, and it's a lot quieter!'

Wesley works in all weathers
Courtesy of Craighead Farm Horse Logging

AT CRAIGHEAD FARM in Ayrshire, Ken Stewart is an enthusiastic promoter of the horse for woodland and forestry management. He and his Clydesdale, Wesley, provide felling and cutting services in environmentally sensitive areas, demonstrating the low impact advantages of horse logging. As fuel costs escalate, the attraction of horse power is growing and Ken also offers training courses on horse logging to complement woodland management courses. Typically, Wesley also has his own fan club and is welcomed everywhere he goes. For many businesses, Clydesdale horses are the best public relations ambassadors, especially when they are earning their keep into the bargain.

Clydesdales stables at Millisle, Garlieston,
Wigtownshire
*Courtesy of Hugh Ramsay, Photo Nancy
Anderson*

Harness room at Millisle, Garlieston, Wigtownshire
Courtesy of Hugh Ramsay, Photo Nancy Anderson

Horse Tram, Douglas,
Isle of Man
Photo Douglas C. Dodd

IN DOUGLAS, Isle of Man, the oldest surviving Horse Tramway in Britain is drawn by Clydesdale horses. In total the Douglas Bay Tramway has 30 horses, each which works six days a week from May to September, providing a service which has operated continuously since 1876, excluding World War II. A fleet of over 20 tram cars, owned by Douglas Corporation, are stored at the Derby Castle sheds, while the horses are housed during the season in the stables at the bottom of Summer Hill. Popular with visitors during the tourist season, they can also be seen in winter participating in one of the many ploughing matches held on the island.

Training a tram horse, Douglas, Isle of Man
Photo Douglas C. Dodd

In the past the Corporation had its own breeding programme, introduced forty years ago when the cost of purchasing horses had almost doubled over the course of one year. Their first foal was born in 1974, and their last foal, Debbie, was bred in 1999. Their horses are now bought as yearlings from the Ballafayle Stud at Maughold, on the island, and at any one time there will be nine or ten young horses growing up and in training. Broken in at four years old, they can have a working life of eighteen years or more.

Victor Harbour Horse Drawn
Tram, South Australia
*Courtesy of Victor Harbour
Tramway*

The Douglas Tramway has historic links with a similar service in Victor Harbour, on the Fleurieu Peninsula, South Australia. Established in 1894, the Victor Harbour Horse Drawn Tram runs a year round service of double deck trams, pulled by Clydesdale horses, over a 630 metre wooden causeway to Granite Island. As well as the regular public tram service, group bookings are taken for special events.

The seven Clydesdales graze on 50 acres of pasture by the Inman River. On a normal working day, three will go to work while the others rest. Every morning at 7.30 they all gallop up to the stable paddock for a breakfast of Lucerne hay, 'a daily race just for the fun of it'. Ian Williams is the Co-ordinator, who takes responsibility for the training and management of the horses as well as driving the trams. He and the team ride the horses to work each day, enjoying a shoreline wade along the way. And on 1st August each year, the official birth date of horses in the Southern Hemisphere, they hold a Horse's Birthday Celebration complete with a large carrot cake cut by the Mayor of Victor Harbour.

IN THE CITY of Glasgow, the Cleansing Department replaced their Clydesdales with lorries in 1956, but the Parks Department continued to use Clydesdales for parks maintenance until the late 1960s. But Glasgow folk had never forgotten the heavy horses, and in June 1983, they were re-introduced in Glasgow Green as part of the 'Glasgow's Miles Better' Campaign. Bobby Woods, who had been Head Carter with Black & White Whisky until their stables were closed, was appointed to take charge of 'Pete' and 'Jock' at the stables next to the People's Palace.

Willie Sheret and Liz Mulligan with Rocky, the City of Glasgow entry at the Royal Highland Show 1993
Sheret family collection

The move was so popular that, in 1990, Clydesdales were returned to Pollock Country Park, with 'Rocky' and 'Ranger' and Willie Sheret, an experienced horseman who was also a well known show jumper, became Head Carter.

The popularity of the horses with the public can be in no doubt. As the drays travel around the parks and the city streets, smiles break out on the faces of young and old alike. When the annual Santa's dray rides are announced, they sell out within three days.

City of Glasgow Clydesdales at Pollok House, Glasgow, 2010
Glasgow City Council Land and Environmental Services

A real public relations success for the City of Glasgow, the Clydesdales have travelled beyond the city to win both driving and ridden prizes at major agricultural shows. In 2010, Head Carter Lorraine Clark rode ILPH Baron to win the Ridden Class at the Royal Highland Show.

Baron is himself a success story. He was one of 30 horses rescued by the International League for the Protection of Horses (now World Horse Welfare) when the Fairways Heavy Horse Sanctuary in Perthshire closed in 2000. He came to Glasgow in 2001 as a five year old, with his stable mate Mac, and is a great advertisement for the World Horse Welfare Loan Scheme as he represents the City of Glasgow on a daily basis.

World Horse Welfare have also loaned a 19 hands seven year old Clydesdale gelding to the Household Cavalry in London to train as a potential drum horse. It takes two years to undergo the thorough assessment and training to enable a horse to carry 90 pound drums plus a 200 pound rider, and to remain calm and still amid flashing lights, loud noises and large crowds. Drum horses have their manes, tails and feathers untrimmed, and are guided by foot reins.

Claude in Valley Field at Osborne
House, Isle of Wight
Courtesy of Osborne Carriages

CLYDESDALES have recently returned to Osborne House on the Isle of Wight many years after they were originally brought to the island by Queen Victoria and Prince Albert in 1845. At Barton Manor Farm, neighbouring Osborne House, Prince Albert invested in the development of the estate and built new farm buildings which included stables for thirteen horses, most of which were Clydesdales. The horses worked on the estate in teams, and a measure of Albert's enthusiasm for the breed is shown in that Glenelg, the prize winning stallion, stood at stud there. Interestingly, Glenelg was the sire of Cumberland, the first Clydesdale imported into Canada in 1840.

Courtesy of Osborne Carriages

Beverly Knight and Lea Western decided to re-introduce the breed in 2009 when they took over the business of carriage rides on the estate. They saw the opportunity to re-establish the tradition of having these famous Scottish horses on the royal estate after more than a hundred years. The first one they acquired was Claude, an 18.1 hands strawberry roan who had been rescued after being abandoned in a field. Nursed back to

Reilly and carriage in the grounds
of Osborne House, Isle of Wight
Courtesy of Osborne Carriages

health at stables in Cumbria, he arrived at Osborne House to continue his recovery and begin his training as a carriage horse. A matching 17.3 hands strawberry roan, Reilly, arrived a few months later from Suffolk. Reilly had already done some carriage work and was quickly at work taking visitors from the reception area to the main house.

Jayne Chapman working
Mardoug's Benmore at Tatton Park
Home Farm, Knutsford, Cheshire
Courtesy of Cheshire East Council,
Tatton Park

Tatton Park Clydesdales
demonstration at Cheshire
County Show
Courtesy of Cheshire East
Council, Tatton Park

Headowork Apple Blossom with one hour old colt foal, Tatton Grey Friar
Courtesy of Cheshire East Council, Tatton Park

AT TATTON PARK Home Farm, near Knutsford in Cheshire, the Clydesdales are hugely popular personalities with the public. The geldings are used for demonstrations where they are converted from driven to ridden, and the demos finish with the pair being ridden to a piece of classical music. The mare, Headowork Apple Blossom, has bred four foals. One is in Sweden, one in Germany, and her filly is still on the farm due to be put in foal in 2011. Jayne Chapman confirms that they are committed to promoting the Clydesdales and demonstrating their versatility as part of the authentic working farm.

Clydesdales Across America Tour, 2005

CAPABLE of hard work and with incomparably gentle natures, the Clydesdale is hugely popular today wherever transportation and public relations can be used to combined advantage. The world's best known example is Budweiser, whose Clydesdales have become global icons which have become the instantly recognisable ambassadors for Anheuser-Busch beers for over 75 years. In 2005 'Clydesdales Across America: Here's to the Heroes' was a nation wide tour in tribute to America's armed forces. Two eight horse hitches set off on April 22nd, one from New York and the other from San Francisco, visiting 22 cities along the way. They finally met in St. Louis on July 4th, where they were the hosts to a huge Independence Day celebration light show. The tour was so popular, in fact, that it was extended twice and finally ended in Philadelphia in December.

Each year, seven teams of Clydesdales tour the United States for most of the year, making more than 500 appearances. Anheuser Busch own more than 250 Clydesdales, and run two breeding facilities where up to 40 foals are born each year. The original is Grant's Farm, St. Louis, and in 2009 a brand new 350 acre breeding farm was opened in Cooper County, Missouri.

A NOVEL venture can be found in Australia, where the Clydesdale is known as 'the world's best loved draught horse'. In Windsor, New South Wales, the world's first horse drawn restaurant, Clydesdales Restaurant, was launched in 1995. Three Clydesdale horses pull a completely refurbished 1890s omnibus, offering breakfast and lunch tours on Sundays and dinner tours on Saturdays and weekdays. Bookings are taken for private use, and weddings are popular.

In Fremantle, Western Australia, Clydesdale Dining have a fully enclosed dining carriage pulled by two Clydesdales, visiting local tourist attractions while up to 15 guests enjoy a three course meal. The ambience and the food may be special in these unique dining experiences, but the Clydesdales are the main attraction with the customers.

Horses Charlie, Andre and Banjo make a special wedding. Clydesdales Restaurant, Windsor, New South Wales, Australia
Courtesy of Clydesdales Restaurant

Farrier Jim Ferrie shoeing a
Clydesdale at the Millennium Horse
Show, Kittochside, South
Lanarkshire, 2000
Photo John Zawadzki

Scotland's beautiful heavy horse is loved and worked in the twenty first century, in locations all over the world. His popularity grows as more and more people find new and different ways of using his strength, agility, and willing temperament.

In 2003, the late Charlie Pinney made an impassioned plea in a lecture entitled 'Real Live Horse Power'. In the second decade of this century, it seems that some, at least, have heard him.

'Living horse power is cheap and readily available. We can breed horses, without limit, without endangering the planet. We know a lot about them and how to use them. They can pull things for us, carry us, help support our society, feed it and enable it to function. They can do so far better than they did in the past if we take advantage of some of the technical advances made in agriculture and machinery design. They can be fed from our fields. They don't destroy the environment but enhance it. They create employment, not replace it. They are a source of companionship in the workplace, a source of pride and pleasure when seen to be working to perfection in harmony with man and his surroundings. Why on earth don't we use them?'

Ploughing with a 6-horse team and a 3 furrow Reid and Grey plough at Cottle's farm, Timaru, New Zealand
Courtesy of the Cottle family

Cathcart Lofty and Samantha Weir mustering
Aberdeen Angus cattle, Goulburn, New South
Wales, Australia
Courtesy of Samantha Weir

Colt foal
Courtesy of the Cottle family

ACKNOWLEDGEMENTS

This book was made possible by the kindness and generosity of a great many people, who gave me their time, shared their precious memories and photographs and encouraged me every step of the way. Some asked not to be named. They too are offered my heartfelt thanks. You know who you are! Especially, too, I want to thank my husband Stan for his patience and forbearance as our house became a repository for a large accumulation of Clydesdale material.

John and Jacqueline Adamson, Julie Affleck, Nancy Anderson, Janet Bain, Robin Barr, Richard, Duke of Buccleuch and Queensberry KBE, Neil Bruce, Alison Burgess, Sue Butterick-Kent, Don Carney, Charles Carrick, Lorraine Clark, Nancy Cook, Hamish Cottle, William Crawford, Michael Crellin, Angela Davidson, Douglas Dodd, John Dodd, Bob Donnachie, Pamela Duncan, John Dunlop, James Edgar, James Emmons, Frederic and Noemie Faure, Jim Ferrie, Tom Fountain, Neil Fraser, Chris Frear, Aileen Gardiner, Sara Geisner, Lindsay Gemmell, Alasdair Govan, Rev. Sandy Gunn, Gordon Hedley, Jenny Henderson, Sir David Hope-Dunbar BT , Ed and Edna Hunter, Pat Hunter, Jim Irving, Tomas and Sofie Jonsson, Danny Kerr, David Kett, Beverly Knight, May Lockhart, John McMillan, Jim McNay, Jane Marchbank, Bob Marshall, Catriona Melvin, Moira Methven, Marilyn Muir, Morag Murray, Sheila Murray, Marguerite Osborne, Sally Ann Oultram, Jim Poole, Jamie Quinn, Hugh and Margaret Ramsay, Alan Reed, Alan Reid, Irene Riddall, Graham Roberts, Lesley Ronald, Neill Ross, Bruce Roy, Andy Scott, Willie Sheret, George and Ruth Skinner, Jonathan Smith, Jim Steel, Donald Smith, Jim and Eileen Thomson, Tom, Marjory and Peter Tennant, Yvonne Thackeray, Bill Todd, Tom Tweedie, Ian Wade, George Walker, Hilda Wallach,

Anne Waugh, Samantha Weir, Lea Western, Louise Wilsden, David, Frances and Richard Wise, Jerry and Barbara Wismer, Victor Wilson, Marion Young, John Zawadzki.

The resources and assistance of the following have been invaluable:

Aberdeen City Council Libraries and Archives, Anheuser-Busch Incorporated, A.G.Barr plc, Bibliographic Data Services Ltd., Chivas Brothers, Robert D. Clapperton Photographic Trust, Clydesdale Breeders of the USA, Clydesdale Horse Association of Canada, Clydesdale Horse Society, Clydesdale Horse Society of New Zealand, Commonwealth Clydesdale Horse Society of Australia, Diageo Brands BV, Dudley Archives, Dumfries and Galloway Libraries and Archives, Dundee City Council Libraries and Information Services, East Dunbartonshire Council Libraries and Archives, City of Glasgow Land and Environmental Serices, Glasgow Museums Service, Glenbow Archives, Midlothian Council Library Service, Moray Council Libraries and Information Services, National Co-operative Archive, National Library of Scotland, National Museums of Scotland, Orkney Library and Archive, Perth and Kinross Libraries and Archives, The Ronald Duncan Archive, Royal Highland and Agricultural Society Library, Scotsman Publications Ltd., Scottish Farmer, Scran Ltd., The Timaru Herald, Whithorn Photographic Group.

Grateful thanks are due to the following for coyright permissions granted:

Catherine J. Reid for the work of the late Will H. Ogilvie, Mrs Ann Davidson and the family of the late Geordie Rodger, Graham Garson and the family of the late J.G.S. Flett, Alysoun Neill on behalf of the family of the late William Neill, the family of the late George Corrigall, Allan Wallace for his poem *A Debt that can never be repaid,* Robert M. Banks for *The Quarry Horse,* and A.P. Watt Ltd. on behalf of Timothy d'Arch Smith for Gilbert Frankau.

Every effort has been made to trace copyright holders and we apologise for any unintentional omission. We would be pleased to insert the appropriate acknowledgement in any subsequent edition.

BIBLIOGRAPHY

Angus, D. *Clydesdale and working horses* Axiom Australia 2008

Baird, E. *The Clydesdale horse* B.T. Batsford 1982

Bowden, C. *The last horsemen* Andre Deutsch 2001

Brereton, J. *The horse in war* David & Charles 1976

Chivers, K. *The Shire horse* J.A. Allen 1976

Clydesdale Horse Society Stud Books, various volumes

Davies, J. *Tales of the old horsemen* David & Charles 1997

Diehl, D. *The great American tradition* Anheuser-Busch Inc. 2008

Fraser, A. *The native horses of Scotland* John Donald 1987

Galtrey, S. *The horse and the war* Country Life 1918

Kilpatrick, J. *My 70 years with Clydesdales* Munro 1949

Neat, T. *The horseman's word* Birlinn 2002

Nimmo, I. *Scotland at war* Archive Publications 1989

Paget-Tomlinson, E *The railway carriers* Terence Dalton 1990

Roberts, D. *For to do the country good* Strathkelvin Council 1987

Shaw, M. *Clydesdales* Great American Pub. 2005

Statistical Account of Scotland various volumes

Weatherley, L. *Great horses of Britain* Spur Publications 1978

Whitlock, R. *Gentle giants* Lutterworth Press   1976

Wright, R. *Standard Cyclopedia of Modern Agriculture* Vol. 3 Gresham 1911

Periodicals

The Clydesdale International, Middleholm Farm, Lesmahagow, South Lanarkshire, ML11 0HL, various issues

The Draft Horse Journal, PO Box 670, 2700 Fifth Avenue NW, Waverly, Iowa 50677, various issues

Heavy Horse World, Lindford Cottage, Church Lane, Cocking, Midhurst, West Sussex, GU29 0HW, various issues

Poppy, aged 4 weeks, with her dam Udale Jenz

APPENDIX

A special acknowledgement

The photograph of the Clydesdale with grass sickness in Chapter 4 was used by the very kind permission of Jenny Henderson, the owner of Udale Poppy who went down with this disease in 2006. This is her story.

Poppy, by Greendykes Northern Star out of Udale Jenz, was born in 2005 and shown successfully as a foal and a yearling, and entered for the Royal Highland Show in 2006.

But early in June of that year Jenny noticed that something wasn't right. Poppy had muscle tremors at the top of her front leg and patches of sweat on her shoulders. Although she was eating and her temperature was normal, over the next few days her symptoms got worse; she was 'gripped up' and not finishing her feeds.

When the vet made the tentative diagnosis of grass sickness he told Jenny to encourage Poppy to eat anything she wanted. 'I cleared the shelves of carrots and apples in Tesco!' she said.

But the deterioration continued and the decision was taken to send Poppy to the Dick Vet Hospital in Edinburgh, 200 miles from Jenny's home in the Black Isle, north of Inverness.

She had lost 70 kilos of her 550 kg weight in nine days, and the specialist care provided by the dedicated veterinary staff in Edinburgh seemed to offer her best chance of recovery.

Over the next six weeks Poppy lost another 100 kilos, in spite of the best efforts of the vets and the grass sickness nurse who tried everything to encourage her to eat. In mid July Jenny received a phone call to say Poppy had gone down and was unable to get up. She made the long journey to see her, thinking it would be for the last time. But to her amazement, Poppy had managed to stand up by the time Jenny arrived, although she was very weak. The vets inserted a stomach tube, and Poppy was fed Ready-brek for the next two days.

When the tube was taken out, Jenny led her out onto the grass outside the stable. Poppy looked around for a minute or two, and then put her head down and slowly started grazing. From then on, she began to improve and gain weight. She had been at the Dick Vet Hospital for three and a half months when Jenny took her home, weighing 420 kilos.

Three months later her weight had returned to 575 kilos, and at the Royal Highland 2007, Poppy was placed third in a very strong class of 2 year old fillies.

Although recovery from grass sickness is not unheard of, it is very rare. This is a tribute to Jenny and Poppy, and the efforts of everyone involved at the Dick Vet Hospital and the Equine Grass Sickness Fund.

Poppy at the Dick Vet Hospital, July 2006

Poppy at the Highland Show, June 2007

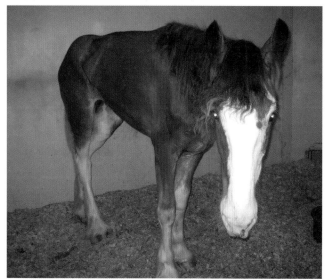

Index